Pedographs and Gait Analysis:
Clinical Pearls
and
Case Studies

Edited By Ivo Waerlop
Editorial assistance by Shawn Allen

North America & international
toll-free: 1 888 232 4444 (USA & Canada)
fax: 812 355 4082

To Our Patients,
whom we learn from every day

Table of Contents

6

Foreword

How is a loaf of bread the mother of an airplane? Necessity is the mother of invention. This book arose out of necessity. There are scientific papers which mention pedograph usage and brief homilies in books, but through our combined clinical experiences, we have not been able to find a comprehensive source for pedograph analysis. It is such a simple tool, both educationally and clinically, yet it seems to be grossly underutilized, thus the need for a text (of sorts).

I can remember the 1st time I saw a pedograph used. It was during my 1st orthotic evaluation with a pedorthist that worked in my office. Of course, I had perfect feet, and didn't need orthotics, or so I thought. Foot mechanics at that time were foreign to me (other than mechanoreceptors), and all problems existed in the receptor, effector, peripheral nerve, spinal cord, brainstem, cerebellum, thalamus or cerebrum. Well my Morton's style foot, along with internal tibial torsion really were the root of my knee pain, and thus the journey began.

A short time later, I began to learn more about foot mechanics on my own, mostly through reading Tom Michaud's text, and continued to employ pedorthists in my office. This is when I first met Shawn Eno. We cross referred some patients and the world was a great place to live in.

Two years and another office later, I was badgered by a good friend to attend a seminar on orthotics and foot biomechanics by Dr. Ed Glaser. I finally remitted and went, just to make my friend happy. The seminar had a lot of good information, despite the bad jokes. I started reading more... and more...

and more. I soon became a shoe nerd and started giving seminars at my local shoe stores and ski shops on proper shoe selection, foot and ankle biomechanics, and boot fit. My wife thought I was very strange, hanging out in the shoe department of any store we visited and talking about things like dual density midsoles and torsional rigidity. Soon after I began teaching the material on a post graduate level, and thought I was pretty good. That's when I began hanging out with and having in depth conversations with Shawn Eno, and realized that I only had a primitive understanding of what was really happening during the gait cycle. This is when my real education began, as I learned to analyze, digest, post, change and modify orthotics. I really feel sorry for my first few patients that I worked with. You know what I am talking about, as you often see your "work" months or years later from when you started and ask yourself how this person was actually able to walk on this and not get worse. Most of my patients are very understanding (and forgiving) people and thus they have allowed me to "learn" on them. I've improved greatly, but strive to learn more each day.

I had heard of this elusive fellow, an instructor from National College, whom I had never met. We spoke briefly on the phone a few times and he seemed to know what he was talking about. Shawn and I were starting a consulting company and he said that this other guy, Dr Shawn Allen, would be a good addition. Having been an Instructor at NYCC and various colleges myself, I figured he was probably a bright guy, though probably an academic. I met Shawn Allen at our first lecture in Chicago at National University of Health Sciences. He was very formal (as predicted) in his 3 piece suit (I was Colorado casual, chino's, shirt, tie and sneakers). I did my thing and thought I came off pretty well. That is of course, until I heard Shawn Allen speak. In short, he blew my sox off. Guess it doesn't pay to profile people. (Incidentally, he has loosened his dress code)

Thus, our relationships were forged and the beginning of this text became a reality. I feel very fortunate to have such gifted lecturing partners. We all have our strengths (and weaknesses), and as a result, we are able to deliver an extremely comprehensive educational message to our audiences. We continually learn from each other and our patients.

This book/monograph is constantly evolving. Though the gait cycle doesn't really change, our understanding of it does as research and the knowledge base expands.

We hope that you find this material as enjoyable as we do, and if you do, you will probably begin making pedographs of anything that moves, be hanging out in shoe stores, bothering shoe manufacturers for tech manuals and asking shoe manufacturers why they put motion control features in shoes with no torsional rigidity. We hope you become a shoe nerd like us and maybe, just maybe, this book will push you over the edge...

Ivo Waerlop

Introduction

This text is in constant evolution. It actually began 3 years ago when we thought it would be a good idea to write some of these things down, because they weren't available in any one text or paper and in some cases, anywhere, as they are observations we have made either individually or together. What you are looking at is the combined efforts of 3 individual's ideas and learning over many years of teaching, reading, and writing applied to clinical experience. It contains notes, forms, lectures and papers of what we feel are salient points germane to the usage of pedographs. It is by no means all encompassing and information is constantly being added for future editions. We foresee the need for a full gait analysis text with clinical cases, and have begun assembling this for future publication.

To make sense of pedographs, you must have an understanding of lower kinetic chain biomechanics and the gait cycle, and how the two relate to one another. We have skipped basic anatomy and assume that if you are nerdy enough to want to know about pedographs, you already know the basics.

So, in the words of Joey Ramone, *"Hey, ho…Let's go!"*

Pedograph Introduction

 Pedographs were 1st described by Harris and Beath in 1947 (1). It is a rubber mat surface with multiple protruding, small grid lines on one side, which, when covered with ink, imprints an underlying sheet of paper when weight (usually a foot) passes over it. Relative plantar pressures are indicated by the size and density of the inked area (1, 2), creating a "footprint" reflecting gait mechanics at that instance in time. They have fallen into and out of usage over time, often discarded for more expensive technology such as pedobarographs, individual pressure sensors, and pressure sensitive mats, which have nifty computer interfaces and can provide many useful measurements and calculations to assist the clinician with rendering a diagnosis. These systems, though more precise in many ways (provided a controlled, reproducible testing procedure) are often thousands of dollars, require a computer and the necessary skills, and have a substantial learning curve. The pedograph in contrast is simplistic, inexpensive, reliable and merely requires an intact cerebral cortex and knowledge of the events occurring in the gait cycle. In the hands of the expert gait biomechanist, it is quite possible that the subtle nuances detected by the sensitive pedograph (nuances that can be undetected with low end computer driven plantar pressure devices) can offer information quite critical to a precise diagnosis in difficult cases. With minimal training using a pedograph, reproducible "prints" can be produced for analysis, in light of your findings clinically. They also make wonderful educational tools for your patients!

When prescribing orthotics, examination of the entire kinetic chain both in a static and dynamic fashion is essential. Often what you see statically is either directly translated to or compensated for in the dynamic evaluation. The pedograph is a visual tool representing a 2 dimensional image of tridimensional motion, and you are seeing the end product and compensation (or lack thereof) of the individuals mechanics at that point in time. Because of the specificity of what you are seeing refers to a particular point in time, technique and reproducibility are of paramount importance. Prints should be performed several times to insure what you are looking at is what you are looking at, and not movement artifact, because of the way the patient stepped on to or off of the mat.

Bibliography
1. Harris WC, Beath T. Canadian Army Foot Survey, National Research Council, 1947
2. Shipley DE: Clinical Evaluation and care of the insensitive foot. Phys Ther 59(1), 13-18, 1979

Obtaining a reproducible print

In addition to understanding the events occurring in the gait cycle and their resulting plantar pressures, one must be able to record these in a reproducible manner. Having a method or technique with a few constants goes a long way. For example, if the patient steps onto the mat from a greater distance with one foot compared to the other (below left), a heel smear artifact (below right) will be produced, which you may mistake for increased heel pressure or a displaced fat pad.

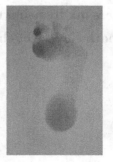

Stepping off the mat to the side (below left), will change forefoot pressures under the metatarsal heads (below right). Note the increased pressure under 1st metatarsal as the patient pushed medially off of the mat instead of progressing forward off of the mat).

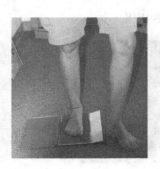

Here is one method of obtaining a print which we have found works well, and is fairly reproducible.

Ink the textured surface of the pedograph and roll out the ink evenly over the entire surface.

Place a piece of pedograph (or less expensive legal paper) paper on the opposite side and bring the hinged canopy down, with the textured side against the paper.

Remove excess ink by using the back of the roller and going over the smooth surface of the rubber a few times.

Flip up the canopy, discard the paper and run the inked roller over the textured side again. Now you will be ready to make prints, and the canopy will only require re-inking on occasion (depending on use). You will need to re-roll the rubber canopy after each print!

Place the pedograph on the floor, preferably on a surface which won't allow the device to slide (carpeting works well, or you can fashion small rubber stops to the bottom of the pedograph).

Have the patient stand barefoot (eliminates sock lines) in shorts, just behind the pedograph (we use a constant 4-6" distance away from the leading edge of the pedograph), with the smooth side of the canopy up and in front of their right foot.

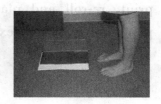

Have the patient step on to the canopy with their right foot. Make sure you are standing to the side or in back of the patient, or you may alter how they step on to the canopy. This point is critical! The patient must not have any conscious or

subconscious perception that there is an obstruction of a free fluid stride across the mat. This is yet another reason why several mappings should be made, to ensure reproducibility and reliability.

Have them "walk through" the pedograph (the opposite leg will be in swing phase) and step off the canopy.

Flip up the canopy, remove the print, re-roll and place another paper down for the next print.

Have the patient turn around, and repeat the previous steps with the opposite foot, while walking in the opposite direction.

Repeat this procedure several times and compare the prints for reproducibility. Compare these findings with your static and dynamic evaluation and draw your conclusions.

Introduction to Dynamic Evaluation of Gait

Gait can be divided into walking gait, jogging gait, and running gait. Each has a different combination of weight bearing and non weight bearing phases.

One gait cycle consists of the events from heel strike to heel strike on one side. A step length is the distance traveled from one heel strike to the next (on the opposite side). Comparing right to left step lengths can give the evaluator insight into the symmetry of the gait. Differences in step length, on the simplest level, should cause the individual to deviate consistently from a straight line (technically it should cause the individual to eventually walk in a large circle!). Most of the time compensations occur functionally in the lower extremities, hips and pelvis to compensate for the differences in step length to ensure gait progression in a straight line. It is these longstanding complex compensations, which are necessary to procure a straight line gait, that are the generators of many of our patient's complaints.

A stride length is the distance from heel strike to heel strike on the ipsilateral side (the distance covered in one gait cycle. Step width is the lateral distance between the heel centers of two consecutive foot contacts (this typically measures 6-10 cm). Foot progression angle is the angle of deviation of the long axis of the foot from the line of progression (typically 7-10 degrees).

Let's begin with a typical walking gait cycle.

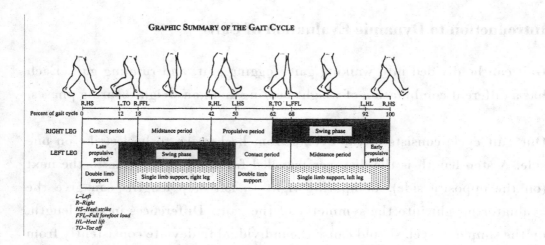

GRAPHIC SUMMARY OF THE GAIT CYCLE

L—Left
R—Right
HS—Heel strike
FFL—Full forefoot load
HL—Heel lift
TO—Toe off

There are 2 phases: stance and swing. Stance can be divided into many phases, depending on your reference source. It comprises approximately 62% of the gait cycle. Inman (2) and Scranton (3) use the following classification:

Heel strike: when the heel hits the ground
Full forefoot load: weight is transferred anteriorly to the forefoot
Heel lift: when the heel begins lifting off the ground
Toe off: the beginning of propulsion

This can be further divided into a contact period (heel strike to full forefoot load), a midstance period (from full forefoot load to heel lift) and a propulsive period (from heel lift through toe off)

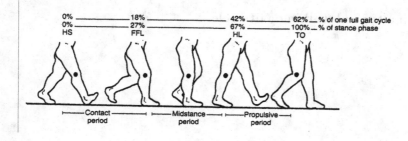

20

Perry (4, 5) uses a slightly more descriptive classification:

Initial contact: when the foot 1st touches the floor

Loading response: weight bearing on the loaded extremity from initial contact and continues until the opposite foot is lifted for swing

Midstance: the 1st ½ of single limb support, beginning when the opposite foot is lifted until weight is over the forefoot

Terminal stance: begins with heel rise and continues until the opposite foot strikes the ground

Pre swing: when initial contact of the opposite extremity begins and toes off ends

She also describes 3 tasks to be performed during a gait cycle: weight acceptance (the limb is able to bear weight), single limb support (when weight is supported by one limb with the other in swing phase), and limb advancement (moving the opposite limb through space to become the next stance phase leg.

The 3 Rockers
According to Perry, progression of gait over the supporting foot depends on 3 functional rockers (4)

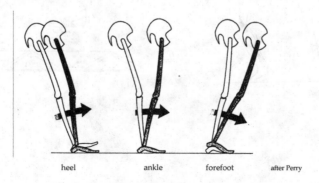

heel   ankle   forefoot   after Perry

21

heel rocker: the heel is the fulcrum as the foot rolls into plantar flexion. The pretibial muscles eccentrically contract to decelerate the foot drop and pull the tibia forward

ankle rocker: the ankle is the fulcrum and the tibia rolls forward due to forward momentum. The soleus eccentrically contracts to decelerate the forward progression of the tibia over the talus. Ankle and forefoot rocker can be compromised by imbalances in strength and length of the gastroc/soleus group and anterior compartment muscles.

forefoot rocker: tibial progression continues and the gastroc/soleus groups contract to decelerate the rate of forward limb movement. This, along with forward momentum (A), passive tension in the posterior compartment muscles (B), active contraction of the posterior compartment (C) and windlass effect of the plantar fascia (D, E, F, G) results in heel lift.

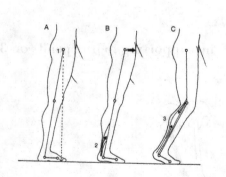
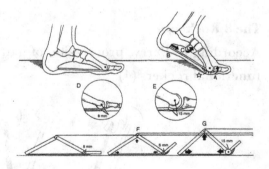

Heel strike, a traumatic deceleration event with the transfer of weight from one extremity to the other, creates shock which must be attenuated. This is accomplished by 4 distinct mechanisms:

1. **ankle plantar flexion** at heelstrike, followed by eccentric contraction of the pretibial muscles to decelerate foot fall.

2. **subtalar pronation.** As the coefficient of friction between the calcaneus and the ground increases, the talus slides anterior on the calcaneus while plantar flexing, adducting and everting. This motion causes concomitant internal rotation of the lower leg. Both these actions cause a time delay, allowing force to be absorbed over a longer period of time.

3. **knee flexion.** This is a reaction to the heel rocker and forward motion of the tibia. It is slowed by eccentric contraction of the quadriceps

4. **contralateral pelvic drop**, which is decelerated by the ipsilateral hip abductors. This occurs as weight is suddenly dropped on the contralateral limb

The rockers and shock attenuation are dependent on the integrity of the joints involved, their associated ligaments and cartilage, the functionality of the musculature crossing them and their neuromuscular integrity along with appropriate cortical control of the actions. Being physical medicine practitioners, we understand that the anatomy and physiology cannot be separated and must consider these different components while evaluating the patient.

Swing phase is less variable in its classification. It begins at toe off and ends at heel strike. It comprises 38% of the gait cycle (1).There must be adequate dorsiflexion of the ankle, and flexion of the knee and hip to allow forward progression.

The following classification is most commonly used (1, 2, 3):
Early swing: occurring immediately after toe off. There is contraction of the dorsiflexors of the ankle, and flexors of the knee and hip

Midswing: halfway through the swing cycle, when the swing phase leg is passing the midstance phase extremity. Acceleration of the extremity has occurred up to this point.

Late swing: deceleration of the extremity in preparation for heel strike. There is contraction of the extenders of the thigh and knee, as well as dorsiflexors of the ankle.

Perry (4) defines the phases as:
Initial swing: the 1st third of swing phase, when the foot leaves the round until it is opposite the stance foot.
Mid swing: the time from when the swing foot is opposite the stance foot until the swinging limb is anterior to the stance phase tibia
Terminal swing: from the end of midswing, until heel strike

Gait evaluation can range from casual observation to treadmill analysis. There is an endless combination of possibilities for explaining what you are seeing, often with many contradictions to what you think should be happening. The best way is to know what normal is supposed to be, observe as many people as possible and try and make clinical correlations based on what you are seeing and what you know. Here are some basics to get you started.

You will need a flat level surface for the person to walk. We feel it is best to evaluate people both with and without footwear.

You don't need a treadmill, but this makes observation much easier since the person is not moving away or toward you. If you're using a treadmill, set it to a 1-2 percent incline (this provides some resistance to forward movement) at a comfortable walking speed (1.5-2.5 miles per hour). A mirror in front of and on one side of the subject allows you to appreciate movement in several planes simultaneously.

Rather than look at the whole picture at once, try and break it down into smaller parts and observe what happens during each phase of gait.

Observe one side at a time.

Look at one joint at a time. Slow motion video (we like Sportsmotion© (7) often helps to be able to see things more clearly.

Marking bony prominences helps as well (we like to use sticky dots found at your local office supply store).

> **Useful markers for gait analysis**
>
> **Posterior**
> Calcaneus
> Distal leg
> 1st sacral tubercle
> PSIS's
> Acromion of scapula
>
> **Lateral**
> Lateral malleolus
> Fibular head
> Greater trochanter
> Center of deltoid
>
> **Anterior**
> Knee caps
> ASIS's

References

1 Root MC, Orion WP, Weed JH. Normal and Abnormal function of the foot. Los Angeles,: Clinical Biomechanics, 1977

2 Inman VT, Ralston HJ, Todd F. Human Walking. Baltimore, Williams and Wilkins, 1981

3 Scranton PE, et al. Support phase kinematics of the foot. In Bateman JE, Trott AW (eds). The Foot and Ankle. New York, Thieme-Stratton, 1980

4 Perry J. Gait Analysis: Normal and Pathological Function. Thorofare, NJ, Slack 1992

5. The Pathokinesiology Service and the Physical Therapy Department. Observational Gait Analysis. Rancho Los Amigos National Rehabilitation Center Downey, CA 2001

6. Michaud T. Foot Orthoses and Other Forms of Conservative Foot Care. Thomas Michaud Newton, MA 1993

7. www.Sportsmotion.com

Walking Gait Summary

There are 2 phases of gait: *stance and swing*.
Stance is divided into 2 parts: *Weight acceptance and single limb support*
Weight acceptance is divided into 2 parts: *Initial contact and loading response*
Single limb support has 3 parts: *midstance, terminal stance and preswing*

Swing has 1 part: *swing limb advancement*
Swing limb advancement is divided into 3 parts: *initial swing, midswing and terminal swing*. These will be discussed in a later section.

> **Stance Phase**
> Initial contact
> Loading response
> Midstance
> Terminal stance
> Preswing

Weight acceptance phase: Initial Contact (heel strike)
During initial contact the foot should strike the ground in a slight supination with the ankle neutral or dorsiflexed. The heel should contact the ground at approximately a 17° angle from the center of the heel. The friction between the heel and the ground should initiate pronation as the calcaneus stops and the talus continues to slide forward sequentially engaging each subtalar facet joint. The knee is neutral or slightly flexed and the hip is flexed 20-30°. There is a momentary contraction of the popliteus muscle to assist the posterior cruciate ligament in attenuating anterior translation of the femur on the tibia.

29

Significant events occurring at heel strike:

Ankle
Supinated slightly (forefoot inverted 8 degrees)
Dorsiflexed slightly
Toe out slightly (6 degrees)
Knee
Femur slightly adducted (2 degrees) with weight coming over
Knee extended
Pelvis
Raised slightly (1" or less)
Rotated slightly backward (2 degrees)
Arms
Ipsilateral arm extended, contralateral flexed

Weight acceptance and loading response
Pronation should begin as the talus slides forward on the anterior facet of the calcaneus as it plantar flexes, adducts and everts. This lowers and deepens the ankle mortise, allowing shock to be attenuated over a longer period of time. Subtalar joint range of motion is increased because the axes of the talonavicular and calcaneocuboid joints become parallel. Some believe that the subtalar joint range is generous at this point because the talonavicular joint, having a concave-convex ball and socket relationship,

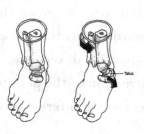

Talus adducts, plantar flexes and everts

30

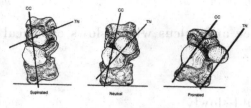

Talonavicular and calcaneocuboid joint axes become parallel.

has an infinite number of axes of motion due to this sphericity. Hence, any axis of the calcaneocuboid joint will have a matching and corresponding axis with the talonavicular joint thus keeping them parallel and thus unlocked and mobile. The total range of motion is in the vicinity of 4-12°.

The downward force of the body causes the calcaneus to evert for 2 reasons:
1. the center of gravity is medial to the calcaneus at this time
2. the adduction and eversion of the talus causes internal rotation of the lower limb (and thus talus internal rotation), which rotates the calcaneus externally (into eversion). The internal rotation of the lower leg causes the knee to flex approximately 20° and allows the quadriceps to help dampen forces while eccentrically contracting. This contraction assists hip flexion through action of the rectus femoris.

We are often on a mission to "stamp out all pronation". Though overpronation has pathological sequela, remember that some pronation is necessary for normal gait. It is a shock absorbing mechanism, along with plantar flexion of the ankle, flexion of the knee and contralateral drop of the hip.

The amount of calcaneal eversion will be limited by the range of motion of the subtalar and calcaneocuboid joints, eccentric contraction of the posterior compartment (tibialis posterior, flexor digitorum and flexor hallicus longus

31

to slow pronation and the medial gastroc and soleus which slows calcaneal eversion)

The ankle plantar flexes 5-10 °and should slowly be lowered to the ground by eccentric contraction of the anterior compartment muscles (tibialis anterior, extensor digitorum and extensor hallicus). This serves to limit stress to the plantar tissues and attenuate shock. This motion represents *heel rocker*.

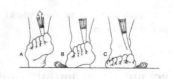

Heel rocker revisited

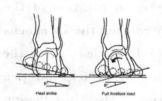

The foot strikes the ground in 8° inversion and is brought to ground through continued subtalar pronation. The tibialis anterior dorsiflexes and inverts the foot at heel strike while the EDL and peroneus tertius dorsiflexes and evert the foot. Both help to maintain the midtarsal joint pronated about its oblique axis while smoothly lowering the foot to the ground while eccentrically contracting.

Heel strike to full forefoot load (loading response to midstance)

Ankle
Calcaneal eversion to max of 4 degrees at full forefoot load
Ankle moving into plantar flexion
Beginning of subtalar pronation and eversion of foot

Knee

Femur adducting

Knee flexing slightly

Pelvis

Leveling to 0 degrees

Rotating forward

Arms

Ipsilateral arm flexing, contralateral extending

Single limb support phase: midstance and terminal stance

Midstance to terminal stance

Midstance should be the mid point of stance phase. The subtalar joint should be fully pronated, limited by it's own range of motion, the range of motion of the calcaneocuboid joint, the amount of calcaneal eversion available along the passive tension medial gastroc/soleus, tibialis posterior, flexor hallicus longus and flexor digitorum. It is the transitional point when the opposite extremity should be

> **Factors controlling pronation at midstance**
>
> ROM of subtalar joint
> ROM of calcaneocuboid joint
> Eccentric contraction of posterior compartment
> Ligamentous integrity of the ankle mortise and midtarsal articulations

entering swing phase which helps to initiate supination of the stance phase foot. The mid point of ankle rocker occurs here.

The forward progression of the tibia is attenuated by eccentric contraction of the posterior compartment, especially the tricep surae. Sometimes, the anterior compartment will be utilized concentrically to help to "pull the body over the ankle", particularly if heel and foot strike is far anterior to the center of gravity of the body as it often is in running gait.

Full forefoot load

Ankle
Calcaneal eversion to max of 4 degrees
Ankle maximally pronated at 8 degrees
Ankle moving into dorsiflexion
Knee
Femur adducting
Knee flexing to max of 20 degrees
Pelvis
Dipping to 2-4 degrees
maximally forward
fully adducted over stance phase leg, movement not > 4 cm
Arms
Moving toward neutral
Terminal stance

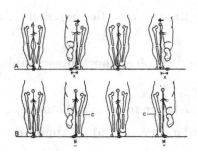

What's the lateral column?

The lateral column consists of the calcaneocuboid joint and its associated metatarsals and phalanges.

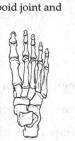

This represents the time from midstance to heel rise. Ankle rocker continues and resupination of the stance phase foot with locking of the lateral column are requisite for proper mechanics. The ankle is now dorsiflexing to approximately 5°, limited by passive tension in and eccentric contraction of the posterior compartment. The quadriceps are concentrically contracting to extend the knee in preparation for

34

toe off and the popliteus contracts to help the now externally rotating femur to keep pace ahead of the externally rotating tibia. If this doesn't happen, it creates a conflict at the femoral tibial joint causing maceration of the meniscus (an unfortunate byproduct of over pronation and inadequate resupination). The hip extends 10 ° from forward momentum of the body and concentric contraction of the hamstrings and gluteals, being slowed by eccentric contraction of the iliopsoas and rectus femoris.

The calcaneocuboid locking mechanism
Locking of the lateral column of the foot is a necessary prerequisite for normal force transmission through the foot and ultimately placing weight on the 1st ray for proper toe off. Locking of the lateral column minimizes muscular strain as the muscles (soleus, peroneus longus and brevis, EHL, EDL, FDL and FHL) are not strong enough to perform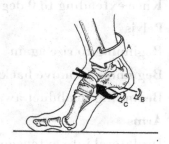
the job on their own. The soleus assists this function by plantar flexing and inverting the subtalar joint, which allows dorsiflexion of 4th and 5th metatarsals and locks the lateral column. It is assisted by the peroneus longus and brevis, which also plantar flex the 1st ray during heel lift and toe off as well as evert (pronate) the forefoot.

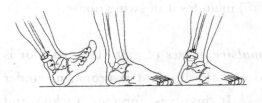 Ankle dorsiflexion at this time gaps and deepens distal tib/fib joint and the fibula drops inferior and externally rotates to deepen the ankle mortise. This serves to provide added stability to the ankle and prevent injury.

35

Full forefoot load to heel lift

Ankle

Calcaneus beginning to invert as opposite leg goes into swing

Ankle beginning to supinate as opposite leg goes into swing

Ankle moving into additional dorsiflexion

Knee

Femur beginning to abduct

Knee extending to 0 degrees

Pelvis

Beginning to rise again

Beginning to move backward

Beginning to abduct away from stance phase leg

Arms

Ipsilateral into extension, contralateral into flexion

Swing limb advancement phase: preswing, initial swing, midswing and terminal swing

Preswing (heel lift and toe off)

Preswing is often included in stance phase, since the foot is still in contact with the ground. Rancho's Los Amigos (5) includes it in swing phase.

Preswing and initial swing are the *propulsive phases* of gait. The rearfoot is supinated, the lateral column is locked and the forefoot is pronating under the influence of the peroneii muscles. It involves forefoot rocker and adequate amounts of dorsiflexion (45° or greater) at the 1st

36

metatarsalphalangeal joint is necessary, or the foot will need to be abducted (most common) or adducted (rare) to accommodate for the lack of range of motion.

As the center of mass of the torso moves forward, the passive tension in series elastic elements of the posterior compartment increase. Simultaneously, there is contraction of the gastrocnemius, which initiates knee flexion and the soleus and deeper muscles of the posterior compartment, which decelerate the forward momentum of the tibia and help to raise the heel by causing plantar flexion. As the torso progresses forward, dorsiflexion of the great toe increases tension in the plantar fascia which assists in maintaining the midfoot in supination and heel rise. This is often referred to as the "Windlass Effect" of the plantar fascia.

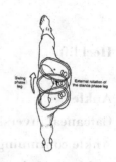

A few words about Peroneus Longus Function in preswing

We remember that the soleus plantar flexes and inverts the subtalar joint, assisting in supination and allowing dorsiflexion of the 4th and 5th metatarsals, in an attempt to lock the lateral column. Ankle plantar flexion puts the soleus at a mechanical disadvantage, decreasing its efficiency. The peroneus longus assists by dorsiflexing and everting the cuboid, locking the lateral column, as well as plantar flexing the 1st ray. Dorsiflexion and eversion is aided by the peroneus brevis and tertius. This causes forefoot pronation which helps to maintain the 1st metatarsal head in contact with the ground.

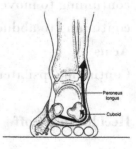

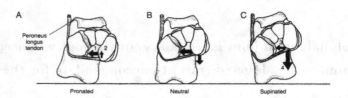

The resultant force of peroneus longus changes with position of the subtalar joint, being flexion downward with supination and actually abduction with pronation

Heel lift

Ankle
Calcaneal inversion

Ankle continuing to supinate

Ankle at 10 degrees dorsiflexion

Knee
Femur abducting

Knee at 0 degrees

Pelvis
continuing to rise

continuing to move backward

continuing to abduct away from stance phase leg

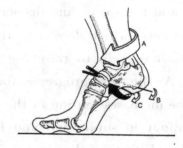

Resupination during terminal stance and preswing to create a rigid lever for propulsion

Arms
Continuing ipsilateral into extension, contralateral into flexion

Heel lift to toe off

Ankle
Calcaneus moving toward eversion

Ankle reaching maximal supination at 4 degrees

Ankle moving into maximal plantar flexion

38

Knee

Continuing to abduct to 0 at toe off

Continuing to flex

Femur at 0 degrees

Pelvis

Moving to 2 degrees raised

Moving to maximally backward

Arms

Ipsilateral into extension, contralateral into flexion

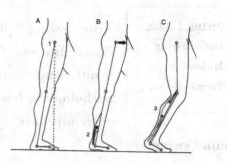

Toe off

Ankle

Calcaneus at 0 degrees

Ankle maximal supination at 4 degrees

Ankle at maximal plantar flexion, 20 degrees

Knee

At 0 degrees abduction

Continuing to flex

Femur at 0 degrees

Pelvis

Raised 2 degrees

maximally backward

Arms

Ipsilateral into max extension, contralateral into max flexion

---

The 4 factors causing heel lift
1. forward momentum of the torso
2. passive tension in the posterior compartment
3. concentric contraction of the posterior compartment
4. Windlass effect of the plantar fascia

39

Swing limb advancement continued: initial, mid and terminal swing

> **Swing Phase**
> Initial swing
> Midswing
> Terminal swing

True swing phase is less variable in appearance. Compensations for leg length discrepancies and muscular insufficiencies are seen here. As a general rule, swing phase pathology is less destructive than stance phase, since the extremity is in open chain.

Initial swing

During initial swing (or preswing) there is contraction of the ankle dorsiflexors, knee and hip flexors to assist the foot in clearing the ground in midswing. The momentum of the swing limb comes from the coordinated action of the plantar flexors of the foot, the contraction of the hip flexors, and the abdominal oblique muscles. The ankle should dorsiflex from 5° to 15°, mostly through the action of the EHL and EDL. The knee rapidly flexes to 60° due to tibial inertia and active flexion of the hip. The activity in the short head of the biceps femoris, sartorius and gracilis peak at this point. This also causes external rotation of the swing phase limb. The iliopsoas, gracilis and sartorius, along with adductor longus create 15° of thigh flexion. It is interesting to note that the sacroiliac joint should remain in 5° extension until midswing. The internal and external obliques help to stabilize the pelvis in the saggital, horizontal and oblique planes and generate some forward momentum of the swing phase leg.

Midswing

This phase is largely passive and is sustained by inertia of the swing phase limb. The ankle should dorsiflex to neutral through the continued action of the TA, EHL and EDL and the foot should clear the ground by approximately 1 cm. Through tibial momentum and eccentric contraction of the biceps femoris, semimembranosus and semitendonosis the knee extends to 25°. The thigh continues to flex to 25°, largely through momentum and the hamstrings begin to contract more at the terminal portion of midswing to slow the leg. The internal and external obliques remain active to stabilize the pelvis and rectus abdominis activity increases ipsi and contralaterally.

Terminal swing
The limb is decelerated, largely through eccentric contraction. The ankle remains neutral and the anterior compartment continues to supinate the forefoot in readiness for heel strike. The knee will extend to neutral and often then flexes 5°. The inertia of the limb continues to extend the knee and the quadriceps contracts concentrically to insure full extension, checked by peak eccentric hamstring activity to decelerate the limb. The thigh falls to 20° of flexion through eccentric activity of the hip flexors. The adductor magnus and lower fibers of the gluteus maximus contract to stabilize and ready the hip for heel strike, checking excessive external rotation. The abdominal obliques, rectus abdominis, rectus femoris, TFL, gluteus medius, and upper fibers of the gluteus maximus begin to contract to provide frontal plane stability at heel strike.

General Swing phase Observations

Ankle
Calcaneus moving toward inversion
Ankle remaining in supination
Ankle moving into dorsiflexion
Knee
Continuing to abduct until midswing, then adducting

41

Continuing to flex to max of 50 degrees just prior to midswing, then beginning to extend

Pelvis

Raising to a max of 4 degrees

Moving forward

Arms

Ipsilateral moving into flexion, contralateral into extension

Walking Gait Observations from a lateral/medial view

The previous section recorded observations from the posterior view. Here are some general observations from the lateral view.

Heel strike to full forefoot load

Metatarso-phalangeal joints

35 degrees dorsiflexion to near

0 degrees

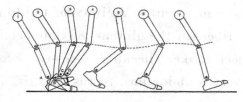

After Perry 1992

Ankle

From slight dorsiflexion to 10 degrees plantar flexion

Pronation proceeds to max

Knee

From extension to 20 degrees flexion

Hip

From 30 to 20 degrees flexion (moving into extension)

Arms

Ipsilateral extension, moving to flexion; contralateral flexion, moving into extension

42

Full forefoot load to heel lift

Metatarso-phalangeal joints
Near 0 degrees
Ankle
From 10 degrees plantar flexion to 10 degrees
dorsiflexion
Supination beginning
Knee
From 20 degrees flexion to almost complete extension
Hip
From 20 degrees flexion to 10 degrees extension
Arms
almost neutral at midstance

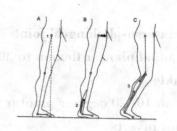

Heel lift to toe off

Metatarso-phalangeal joints
Near 0 degrees to 50 degrees dorsiflexion
Ankle
From 10 degrees dorsiflexion to max of 20 degrees plantar flexion
Maximal supination
Knee
From almost complete extension to 40 degrees flexion
Hip
From 10degrees extension to 0 degrees
Arms
moving to maximal flexion; contralateral moving into maximal extension

43

Swing phase observations

Metatarso-phalangeal joints
Gradual plantar flexion to 30 degrees dorsiflexion
Ankle
From 10- 20 degrees plantar flexion to 0 or slight dorsiflexion
Foot inverts
Knee
Continues to flex to max of 50 degrees at midswing, then to slow extension to near zero at heel strike
Hip
From 0 degrees to 30 degrees extension
Arms
Ipsilateral maximal flexion, moving into extension; contralateral maximal extension moving into flexion

Observations from an anterior view

Heel strike to full forefoot load
Metatarso-phalangeal joints
35 degrees dorsiflexion to near 0 degrees
Ankle
From slight dorsiflexion to 10 degrees plantar flexion
Pronation proceeds to max (8 degrees)
Knee
From extension to 20 degrees flexion
Knee rotates medially (4 degrees femur, 6 degrees tibia)
Pelvis

Rotates anteriorly from neutral to 4 degrees

Adducts across midline, up to 1"

Arms

Ipsilateral extension, moving to flexion; contralateral flexion, moving into extension

Full forefoot load to heel lift

Metatarso-phalangeal joints

Near 0 degrees

Ankle

From 10 degrees plantar flexion to 10 degrees dorsiflexion

Supination beginning just prior to heel lift

Knee

From 20 degrees flexion to almost complete extension

Pelvis

Rotates from 4 degrees posterior to neutral

Begins to abduct from midline

Superior translation to ½", begins to decline

Hip

From 20 degrees flexion to 10 degrees extension

Arms

almost neutral at midstance

Heel lift to toe off

Metatarso-phalangeal joints

Near 0 degrees to 50 degrees dorsiflexion

Foot everts up to 8 degrees

Ankle

From 10 degrees dorsiflexion to max of 20 degrees plantarflexion

Maximal supination

Knee

From almost complete extension to 40 degrees flexion

External rotation to 6 degrees

Hip

From 10 degrees extension to 0 degrees

Pelvis

Rotates from neutral to 4 degrees posterior

Finishes abducting

Pelvis continues to move inferiorly ½"

Arms

moving to maximal flexion; contralateral moving into maximal extension

Swing phase observations

Metetarso-phalangeal joints

Gradual plantar flexion to 30 degrees dorsiflexion

Ankle

From 20 degrees plantar flexion to 0 or slight dorsiflexion

Foot inverts and remains in supination

Knee

Continues to flex to max of 50 degrees at midswing, then to slow extension to near zero at heel strike

Begins internal rotation to prepare for heel strike

46

Hip

From 0 degrees to 30 degrees flexion

Pelvis

Rotates from posterior to neutral

Adducts over opposite stance phase leg

Pelvis continues to move inferiorly ½" then begins to raise just prior to heel strike

Arms

Ipsilateral maximal flexion, moving into extension; contralateral maximal extension moving into flexion

As if all of this isn't enough to think about while observing your patients gait, here are some other things to think about.

Note the angle at which the calcaneus and foot strikes the ground (slightly inverted and toe out approximately 7-10 degrees). The ankle should be dorsiflexed a few degrees. After heelstrike, the calcaneus should evert as the foot lowers to the ground and moves through mid stance into full forefoot load. Note the speed in which eversion and thus pronation is occurring. As the contralateral leg enters swing phase, supination of the weight-bearing leg begins and the arch should start to reappear secondary to 1). Forward progression of the tibia over the leg, 2). Eccentric contraction of the posterior compartment musculature excluding the gastroc/ soleus group, 3). Active contraction of the gastroc/ soleus group during toe off and 4). The windlass effect of the plantar fascia. Watch for excessive contraction of the gastroc/soleus group with people that are over pronators. Observe medial/lateral shifting of the knees during a gait cycle. A person with excessive tibial varum or genu valgum will usually have increased movement.

47

Observe the lateral shift of the pelvis which should not be > 1 inch. If there is a leg length discrepancy, the pelvis usually shifts over the long leg side and the person will appear to be "stepping into a hole" on the short leg side. Observe if there is excessive vertical elevation of the pelvis (>1") during gait cycle. If there is fixation or limited ROM in the ankle, knee or hip will result in this compensation. Now look at the quadratus/erector muscles. Do they contract vigorously at heel strike? This could indicate tight hip flexors and poor eccentric contraction of the gluteus/hamstring with substitution of the erectors. It can also occur with a leg length deficiency (shock attenuation for the long leg side). How is the arm swing? Is it excessive on one side? This will often occur in compensation to lack of forward progression of the contralateral lower extremity.

References
1 Root MC, Orion WP, Weed JH. Normal and Abnormal function of the foot. Los Angeles: Clinical Biomechanics, 1977
2 Inman VT, Ralston HJ, Todd F. Human Walking. Baltimore, Williams and Wilkins, 1981
3 Scranton PE, et al. Support phase kinematics of the foot. In Bateman JE, Trott AW (eds). The Foot and Ankle. New York, Thieme-Stratton, 1980
4 Perry J. Gait Analysis: Normal and Pathological Function. Thorofare, NJ, Slack 1992
5. The Pathokinesiology Service and the Physical Therapy Department. Observational Gait Analysis. Rancho Los Amigos National Rehabilitation Center Downey, CA 2001
6. Michaud T. Foot Orthoses and Other Forms of Conservative Foot Care. Thomas Michaud Newton, MA 1993

Static Evaluation Notes

Static evaluation of the limb is of paramount importance. It gives you a reasonable idea of the ranges of motion available and will help you to understand the compensations which are occurring during the gait cycle. Following is a brief outline of things to look for in your evaluation.

EVALUATION WHILE STANDING

Rearfoot angle: Looking at the way the calcaneus reacts with the ground in a weight bearing posture. It should be neutral to 4 degrees everted. Excessive rearfoot eversion usually occurs with overpronation with compensation; rearfoot varus usually occurs

with a cavus arch, a rigid rearfoot with forefoot compensation. Compare this with your finding prone.

Pronation: Is this occurring at the rearfoot, midfoot or forefoot? Is it to a similar degree bilaterally? Increased pronation often occurs on the side of the longer leg, with relative supination of the shorter side.

Morton's/Bunion/hammer toes: Bunions and hammer toes usually occur in

over pronators. A Morton's toe changes the passage of forces through the foot, putting stress (and thus weight) on the second metatarsal, rather than the first. Their presence signifies a problem. They are formed

49

from the action of the transverse head of the adductor hallicus, in an attempt to stabilize the lateral transmission of forces through the foot. Hammer toes often form in response to overpronation from clawing of the lesser digits in an attempt to gain purchase on the ground, as the foot splays laterally. They both signify a long-standing problem.

Hallux (MPJ) Dorsiflexion (65°): This is important for the toe off phase of gait. The great toe must be able to dorsiflex 40 degrees, otherwise stride length will be decreased due to premature heel rise as the great toe locks early. These folks may experience pain at the first metatarso phalangeal (MPJ) joint 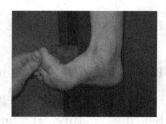 with a posterior spur (sometimes referred to as a dorsal crown of osteophytes) and if chronic and they will have trouble with propulsion, with the inability to transfer weight to the transverse tarsal axis (line between the 1st and 2nd metatarsal) and the foot will be forced to roll off the oblique axis (off metatarsals 3-5). This will be compensated for by flexion at the hip and knee. Incomplete hallux dorsiflexion results in gait/propulsion abnormalities following full forefoot load through toe off. It can also cause great pain at the fixation of the 1st MTP joint, plantar flexion contractures and functional hallux limitus.

It is interesting to note that functional hallux limitus, even to a mild degree, has profound effects on the lower kinetic chain. Even a minor loss of the normal MPJ joint dorsiflexion range can impact the chain. With the loss, the stance phase will be abbreviated via premature heel rise. With early heel rise, propulsion forces will be imparted through a more flexed knee joint generating both translatory shear forces in the saggital plane and torsional

50

forces through the joint proper. Both will cause potential maceration effects on the menisci, but perhaps the greater effects are noted proximally at the hip and pelvis.

It is established on EMG and other studies (Basmajian, Dananberg) that during the open kinetic chain the action of hip flexion is both an active and passive process. The active flexion of the hip is generated largely by iliopsoas concentric contraction. However, this is not the first mechanism to generate hip flexion. In fact, hip flexion is first generated passively through engagement of the kinetic chain (Dananberg). The first movement of the swing phase is rotational / torsional activation of the obliqued pelvis through core activation of the abdominal muscle group. Through activation of the internal and external abdominal obliques and transversus abdominus, in addition to activation of their synergists and co-contraction of their antagonistic stabilizers, the obliqued pelvis is rotated. Better said, the trailing swing leg's hemi pelvis is rotated forward by contraction of the oblique abdominal muscular sling. This forward movement generates a combined saggital and axial momentum; a forward movement of the swing leg. Once initiated, this forward pelvic movement (optimal movements always occur when the core is first stabilized followed by generation of the initial movement of the most proximal limb joint, in this case the hip joint) is translated into passive hip flexion which is then perpetuated by iliopsoas concentric contraction.

In other words, the iliopsoas is not a major initiator of hip flexion, rather, a strong perpetuator of hip flexion. So, when hallux limitus limits the stride length via early generation of heel rise, the maximal pelvic obliquity is lessened. As a result, the degree of initial swing leg movement occurs less from the abdominal activation and thus must be obtained from the hip flexors. The iliopsoas is called upon earlier than desired to assist these efforts thus becoming a hip flexion initiator. Although this demand is minimal, it does not occur without a price. With repetitive demands, thousands of steps

per day, the iliopsoas eventually loses its ability to   Initiation of hip flexion

continue these compensations as does its over-demanded synergists. The result is a possible local hip flexor tendonitis, bursitis, or inhibition due to pain as a result of the undue demands placed upon it. Ultimately the core and low back will suffer once the body's compensatory and protective mechanisms break down and pass the forces beyond the hip joint. It should now be clear that dorsiflexion of the MPJ is critical. Its assessment is imperative and should be compared to the contralateral limb on every examination. With loss of full range of the MPJ, a very common occurrence, the examination should move proximally to the hip and pelvis for a more detailed   assessment   of   compensatory   strategies.

Genu Valgus: the "Q" angle is normally 10-15°. Valgus forces generally

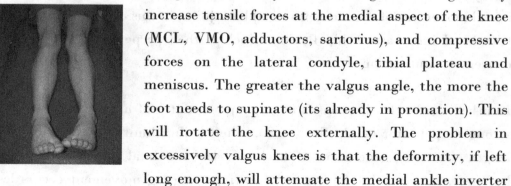

increase tensile forces at the medial aspect of the knee (MCL, VMO, adductors, sartorius), and compressive forces on the lateral condyle, tibial plateau and meniscus. The greater the valgus angle, the more the foot needs to supinate (its already in pronation). This will rotate the knee externally. The problem in excessively valgus knees is that the deformity, if left long enough, will attenuate the medial ankle inverter tendons and medial ligaments and the deltoid ligament complex (increased length over time due to creep as well as stretch weakness) and make appropriate ankle inversion and supination difficult at best. These folks have difficulties decelerating pronatory forces.

Genu Varus: This posturing refers to how "bow legged" the limb measures in the frontal plane. Varus forces increase tensile forces laterally (LCL, VL, TFL) and compressive forces medially on the medial meniscus and medial condyle/tibal plateau. In the varus knee the center of gravity of the body  does not deviate far enough laterally to the stance knee to reduce the lever arms and moments to a non-deforming magnitude. The greater the varus angle, the greater the deforming moments and the more the foot needs to pronate to come into contact with the ground. These folks usually have patellar tracking problems because of the increased internal rotation of the knee.

Genu Recurvatum: This positioning refers to how "bowed" or hyper 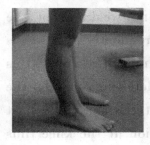 extended the knees are in the saggital plane. The problem can be simple with the excessive motion of hyperextension only at the knee creating the recurvatum or if this joint derangement persists it can lead to a physical bowing of the tibal and fibula in the saggital plane. People often attribute this static postural positioning with excessive soft tissue extensibility or even lax joints but the problem is one of a more complex nature.

Genu recurvatum can be extreme or subtle. One of the main issues with its presentation is that of weakness or stretch-weakness of the gastrocnemius muscle. With this muscle being a two joint muscle crossing proximally over the knee joint, when it is weak or stretched it loses its effectiveness in generating knee flexion, particularly at terminal stance and preswing. Consequently the knee hyperextension is left partially unchecked and there is increased load of the anterior menisci and in children this problem can cause a permanent deformity if left unchecked. If left unaddressed and uncorrected not only can the lower leg bones bow saggitally but the proximal anterior tibial growth plate and anterior articular tibial plateau can deform in a down-sloping or anterior wedged position. This new position will cause further maceration of the anterior menisci, a relative lowering of the patella, patellar tracking problems within the femoral condyles, undue stretch-loading of the posterior cruciate ligament, unloading of the anterior cruciate ligament with possible shortening, a net anterior gliding of the femur on the tibial plateau causing joint malcentration (i.e. it changes the instantaneous axis or "center" of rotation) and reduced activity of the quadriceps extensor mechanism.

In returning to the discussion on weakness or stretch-weakness of the gastrocnemius in recurvatum patients, quite frequently there is compensatory dysfunction within the soleus muscle. In such response, this muscle will become overactive and short and since it is left unchecked by the weak gastrocnemius the soleus will tend to exert a plantarflexion moment at the ankle which will have a resulting effect of extension at the knee thus further engraining the recurvatum issues. This dysfunction can cause further disruption at the ankle. The Achilles tendon can become thick and painful; there can be loss of adequate ankle dorsiflexion, early heel rise and altered eccentric control of tibial progression over the talus during the stance phase of gait (ankle rocker). It is possible this altered tibia-talus relationship can limit terminal dorsiflexion, cause abrupt anterior tibial glide and thus disturb normal or adequate subtalar pronation.

In completing this discussion on saggital plane deviations we would be remiss to neglect a discussion on weakness of the soleus and compensatory shortening of the gastrocnemius. In this scenario the overall tendency for the knee is to present itself slightly flexed and for the ankle to present slightly dorsiflexed. The soleus weakness will allow an unchecked anterior tibial progression over the talus and thus compensation from above in addition to the increased dorsiflexed position at the ankle. These patients will use a quadriceps strategy to stand and ambulate. When walking or running the stride and step length will be reduced and terminal knee extension during heel strike and toe off will not be achieved. The patient will heel strike underneath the body instead of reaching out to lengthen the stride. The knee will remain in flexion and the ankle will remain in relative dorsiflexion the entire gait cycle. Since the soleus has a high composition of slow-twitch muscle fibers (low force application over long durations) it may effectively "survive" most gait adventures unless excessive demand is placed on the limb as in running long distances. In such cases we will see eventual soleus fatigue, pain and spasm.

Heel Walk: The ability to heel walk is a direct reflection on the strength of the dorsiflexors (tibialis anterior, peroneus brevis and tertius, extensor hallicus longus, extensor digitorum longus). Weak dorsiflexors can be a function of tight gastroc/soleus through reciprocal inhibition. This will often result in a "slapping "gait on that side and shin splints from poor eccentric lowering of the foot at heel strike.

Toe Walking: When a person plantar flexes and goes up on their toes, the calcaneii should adduct (invert) due to action of the tibialis posterior. The ability to plantar flex will be dependent on the range of motion of the ankle, amount of great toe dorsiflexion, tightness of the plantar fascia and integrity of the posterior compartment muscles.

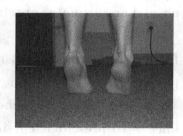

The function of the tibialis posterior is one of ankle plantar flexion, calcaneal inversion and plantar flexion as well as stabilization (through compression) of the first ray complex (talus, medial cuneiform, navicular and base of the first metatarsal). It acts additionally to help decelerate subtalar pronation. Further stabilization of the midfoot comes from smaller tendon slips inserting onto the other cuneiforms, metatarsals, the cuboid and the peroneus longus tendon.

The more common problems that can occur with the tibialis posterior complex are those of muscular strain, tendonitis, tendon insufficiency (stretch) and partial or complete tears. Excessive or prolonged pronation causes excessive dorsiflexion of the first ray complex, increased pronatory effects, and as discussed above, dysfunction of the 1st MPJ joint. The dorsiflexed 1st toe will compromised the efficiency of the windlass mechanism which "winds up" the plantar fascia, properly positions the paired sesamoids, and thus limit effective dorsiflexion of the 1st MPJ. This dorsiflexion of the first ray requires the tibialis posterior to undergo excessive eccentric load for a longer period of time, thus placing more stress on the tendon and muscle belly.

Clinically an individual who has a foot that over-pronates will present with focal tenderness in one or more of the following areas: 1) on the plantar medial aspect of the proximal first metatarsal base, navicular and medial cuneiform; the tenderness representing local insertional tendonitis. This should not be mistaken for plantar fascial pain as the pain does not extend far enough into the plantar aspect of the foot, 2) behind or inferior to the medial malleolus, immediately over the tibialis posterior tendon (this is the area of the tendon which has the most attenuated vascular supply, known as the hypo vascular zone, and thus is an area of slower tendon healing), or 3) local muscular tenderness 2 to 6 inches above the medial malleolus immediately off the medial edge of the tibia (this is the only location where the muscle belly of the tibialis posterior can be even remotely palpated). This is a classic tender spot and good clinical indicator that the tibialis posterior muscle is over challenged. The toe walking is a good screen for the tibialis posterior since ineffective calcaneal inversion is easily noted on single leg stance rising onto the toes. Those of greatest concern for involvement of this muscle are runners/sprinters who over pronate, ballet and figure skaters, individuals who work on ladders such as warehouse shelf stockers, electricians and painters and certainly flat footed individuals.

SEATED EVALUATION & TORSIONS

Tibial Torsion (we will also address some of the mechanics and effects of femoral antetorsion and retro torsion here): This is how much the tibia externally or internally rotates as we develop (in other words, one of the factors which determine if we toe in or out). We are usually born with little or no torsion, and develop 1-1.5° of torsion per year until we stop growing. This ends up being about 22° in the adult (27° transmalleolar angle minus 5° subtalar contribution). Increased torsion forces the foot into pronation faster and causes you to walk on the inside of your foot, altering the transmission of forces through the foot.

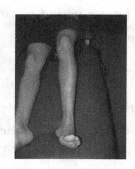

External tibial torsion

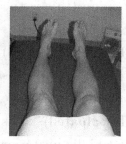

Internal tibial torsion

An effective and simple way to determine if tibial torsion is present is to passively extend the tibia while keeping the knee tracking forward in the saggital plane. If the foot begins tracking a course medially then tibial internal torsion is noted, if tracking laterally then external torsion is noted.

Keep in mind that it is not uncommon for these torsions to be a compensation of a femoral torsion or version (i.e. the angle of the femoral head is altered from its expected anterior orientation of 12-15° with respect to the condyles). Tibial internal torsion can be found as a compensation of femoral retro torsion (femoral head angle <12°) in an attempt to bring the foot into an acceptable progression angle. Similarly, femoral antetorsion (femoral head angle >12°) can be compensated by external tibial torsion.

Keep in mind that these torsional components are complex and will cause complex biomechanics at the hip joint. The compensated femoral antetorsion will compromise hip lateral rotation thus limiting the necessary lateral rotation for normal gait, the lumbar spine will need to laterally flex more than normal to acquire the necessary degree of external rotation.

Compensated femoral retro torsion will limit hip medial rotation and thus compromise the necessary medial femoral rotation required to complete pronation without proximal kinetic chain complication.

Both of these femoral torsional issues will compromise the abilities to adequately eccentrically, concentrically and isometrically control hip rotation demands. Thus, femoral joint centration will be compromised through aberrant roll and glide as seen with the Convex-Concave Rule of ball and socket joints. The body will compensate by attenuating and contracturing various components of the joint capsule; femoral retro torsion will have a short posterior hip capsule and elongated anterior capsule and the ante torsioned hip will have a tight anterior capsule and stretched posterior capsule.

Measuring tibial torsion:

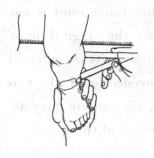

Determining an exact measurement isn't as crucial as determining the effects of torsion, both statically and dynamically. For example, the presence of an internal tibial torsion puts the foot in an adducted posture with the knee in the saggital plane. Most individuals will externally rotate the lower extremity in compensation, often creating a conflict at the knee joint. If an orthotic is now placed under the foot, the knee will be externally rotated further outside the saggital plane, creating a greater conflict. This is often remedied by providing a more forgiving orthotic which allows the individual to pronate through it somewhat and/or utilizing a forefoot valgus post.

For the purists among you, here is how to obtain the measurement. The transmalleolar angle is measured as the angle between the axis of the knee and the transmalleolar axis (drawing a line through the center of the medial and lateral malleoli of the ankle) (see diagram). It is approximately 27°. The talar head rotates externally during development

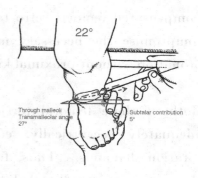

and provides a contribution of approximately 5°. You need to subtract this from the transmalleolar angle to get the true amount of tibial torsion.

more on antetorsion patients:

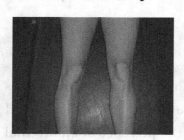

Patients with antetorsion are forced to externally rotate the limbs to bring the feet and knees forward to a normal progression angle. The problem is that the knee hinge joint is not always brought precisely into the saggital plane for unchallenged progression. This external rotation may take up some or all of the lateral rotation needed for the hips to function normally during gait. When this is the case, the patient may be forced to recruit compensatory rotation and/or lateral flexion of the spine.

Normally during gait the hip rotates laterally from shortly after stance phase to slightly after toe off; roughly 10 degrees of lateral hip rotation is necessary to achieve normal toe-off. When this rotation does not occur in the hip, it occurs as a compensatory rotation motion of the pelvis and then at the spinal joints. This abnormal alignment of the femoral head anteriorly in the acetabulum can repetitively irritate the hip joint. Antetorsion patients who compensate and realign the feet to a normal progression angle via tibial external torsion will force the femoral head anteriorly into the anterior hip capsule and this can be a common source of anterior hip/groin pain (as seen in people who sit crossed-legged in the "tailor" position). This is a similar symptom phenomenon as in "anterior femoral glide syndrome" seen in runners and sway back postured patients.

More on retro torsion patients:

In this case, the angle of the head and neck of the femur rotates posteriorly with respect to the shaft. The result is that the range of hip medial rotation appears limited, but the lateral range seems relatively generous because of the deformity.

Retro torsion can also be a source of pain when the limited ranges are challenged. In a patient with retro torsion who also has a foot type that engages excessive pronation (i.e. forefoot varus) pain may result. Retro torsion patients who

force medial rotation can pinch or irritate the anterior capsule and soft tissues (this problem is also seen in individuals with retro torsion who cross their legs, knee over knee). There will be excessive stretch of the hip lateral rotators if medial rotation is forced (sleep can be a problem in these patients if they are side sleepers with the top leg dropping into adduction and medial rotation impinging medial soft tissues). The lateral rotators will be weak representing all 3 phases of muscular weakness (stretch, atrophic and tight).

In the case of bilateral hip retro torsion, the presence of a lack of medial hip rotation causes the lumbar spine to become the site of compensatory motion. Retro torsion is usually compensated with internal tibial torsion in an effort to align the knee into the saggital plane.

In excessively internal tibial torsioned patients the gait strategies are further compromised. These patients should be steered away from a career in running and encouraged to become cyclists, as this causes the foot to remain in more of a supinated posture. These patients have to further enable the internal tibial torsion because they have to bring the retro torsioned femur medially to get the knee to hinge in the saggital plane. This forces them to engage a drastically internally torsioned tibia with the ground. The problem is that they are so far internally torsioned in these cases that if they were to heel strike (laterally, medially or even neutral) they would have their body weight center of gravity so far laterally over the foot that they would frequently inversion sprain the lateral ankle. It will remain difficult for these torsioned patients to bring the knee hinge into the saggital plane and still heel strike appropriately. Thus, these patients who chose to run, must do so with a mid or forefoot initial ground strike and with this their pronation is abrupt, undampened and significant. It is even worse when they have a forefoot varus to contend with at initial contact, the pronation forces in these cases are significantly magnified. The only hope is to put these patients in a well cushioned forefoot shoe, possibly with a gentle forefoot varus (corrective) posting and try to limit their runs to shorter mileage, softer turf, and beg for low-impact cross training.

Tibial varum: This is how much bend (bowing) there is present in the tibia in  the frontal plane. Increased varum will necessitate a steep, medially oriented approach of the foot towards the ground and thus require the foot to pronate through a greater range of motion in a shorter interval of time. This is often accompanied by limited calcaneal eversion (or rearfoot varus) and a cavus foot type, both of which are often developmental in compensation to the tibial varum.

Calcaneal inversion/eversion (20°/10°): The calcaneus must be able to evert at least 4-8° to allow subtalar joint pronation at heel strike; otherwise the subtalar joint must go through a greater range of motion, depending on motion available. If it is unable to pronate enough, compensation must occur elsewhere (transverse tarsal joint, knee, and hip).

Forefoot Flexibility: This is an *extremely general estimate* of the amount of compensation available in the foot as a whole. In part, it will determine how fast or slow the foot will pronate/supinate as well as how good of a mobile adapter it will be. We generally grade this as rigid, normal or hyper mobile.

Ankle plantarflexion/dorsiflexion (35°/15°): Adequate ankle mortise plantar and dorsiflexion is important not only at heel strike, but also at heel lift. These ranges are affected by the integrity of the ankle mortise (talar dome, medial malleolus, and lateral malleolus), to 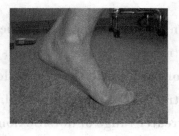 some extent the regional ligaments (contractures/laxity), as well as the gastroc/soleus group (see discussion above on genu recurvatum). It will depend on whether the knee is flexed or extended (increased range of motion with flexion, taking out some of the influence of the gastrocnemius). People who wear heels may have physiological shortening of these muscles and depending on occupation there may be compensatory imbalances (ballet dancers overuse the soleus, electricians on ladders frequently have stretch-weak soleus etc.). The ankle must dorsiflex a minimum of 15°, as this will be required just prior to heel lift: if it is unable to do so, the foot will attempt to pronate more to compensate to achieve the necessary range to propulse. This compensation unlocks the midtarsal joint (calcaneocuboid and talonavicular joint axes become parallel) when forces are peak, which can be damaging to the surrounding structures.

When the range of the ankle mortise joint is compromised by a bony-block range loss the biomechanics must change drastically. In the above example, when dorsiflexion range was lacking, hyperpronation was a possible strategy but for this to occur the tibia must at least progress over the peak of the talus (>50%). In some cases of trauma, where the trimalleolar joint complex has been damaged via tibia-fibula syndesmosis disruption and distal tibia-fibular ligament disruption, a bony end range will be seen limiting the necessary dorsiflexion range required for pronation to adequately occur.

In this case two strategies are possible, a vertical strategy or a medial strategy. In the vertical strategy, the patient will heel strike and progress forward until the bony dorsiflexion block is met, then a plantar flexion strategy can be employed. By plantar flexing the ankle at this point, a greater range of dorsiflexion will again be possible since the tibia will again be positioned more posteriorly on the talar dome. Thus, the patient will plantar flex at the ankle, rising up onto the toes, then the newly provided dorsiflexion range can be utilized. This strategy will allow for forefoot rocker to sufficiently occur to allow forward ambulation but in this case the rocker will occur atop a plantar flexed foot instead of a midstance positioned foot. This strategy is certainly very labored and mechanical, and it will impart an undue amount of abnormal stress on the hips, pelvis and low back, but it does work well.

The second strategy is basically a torsional one in which the patient moves past the limited ankle dorsiflexion range by externally rotating the limb and rolling off of the inside of the foot. The patients only other option is to utilize a rocker bottom sole on footwear and allow the shoe rocker to achieve the ankle ranges needed for forward progression.

EVALUATION WHILE KNEELING

Calcaneal angle (+/- 4°): What is the relative position of the rearfoot, both while weight bearing and non- weight bearing? Ideally, while standing, the calcaneus should be perpendicular to the ground. If the angle is less than 0°, this is

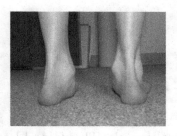

rearfoot valgus

called rearfoot varus. If it is greater than 0°, it is called valgus. This would be the same as rearfoot inversion (supination) and eversion (pronation) respectively.

The rearfoot varus deformity is the most common rearfoot deformity. It is often due to increased tibial varum and/or abnormal subtalar joint development. As a result, the leg is unable to maintain a perpendicular position at heel strike. This results in excessive mid or forefoot pronation that sometimes remains through the propulsive phase (weight passing over an unlocked foot).

Forefoot: What is the forefoot to rearfoot relationship? Forefoot varus means that the forefoot is maintained in an inverted (sometimes called supinated) position. Forefoot valgus means that the forefoot in maintained in an everted (pronated) position. Forefoot varus is more commonly seen. It can be supple (the person is able to compensate fully or to some degree) or rigid (no or little compensation available). A type of rigid compensation for forefoot varus is a plantar flexed 1st

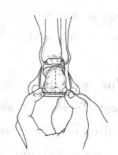

Examining the forefoot to rearfoot relationship

Forefoot varus

A forefoot varus can be compensated or uncompensated. Compensated means that there is adequate motion available in the midfoot or forefoot for the forefoot to reach neutral. Think of the foot as a tripod between the base of the calcaneus and the heads of the 1st and 5th metatarsals. This tripod has perfect balance in a neutral foot or compensated forefoot varus. In an uncompensated varus, one leg of the tripod falls. As a result of a partially or uncompensated forefoot varus, the subtalar joint must pronate through and extreme range of motion to bring the forefoot to the ground. This causes the talus to shift medially (relative to the calcaneus), which maintains the foot in a pronated position throughout midstance and early propulsion (similar to rearfoot varus).This causes a conflict in talar and tibal motions in late midstance/early propulsion (the talus is pronated and medially rotated while the tibia is trying to externally rotate). The stress is most often transferred to the knee, as well as causing laxity of the calcaneonavicular ligament. Thus the calcaneus becomes chronically everted, taxing the associated musculature creating further laxity.

The proximal compensations in the kinetic chain for a forefoot varus are complex. The extreme range of foot pronation needs to be dampened to some degree. Since the compensatory mechanics at the foot, which would normally convert the foot into a supinated rigid structure, are inadequate the challenges move more proximally. The lateral external hip rotators are called upon to eccentrically contract to control the rate at which the limb internally rotates. The problem is that these efforts are frequently inadequate as well and thus lateral hip pain, ilio tibial band or piriformis myofascial problems frequently arise. Another mechanism is an increased demand on the ipsilateral hip adductors concentrically and isometrically to prevent the internal rotation and ensuing genu valgus forces and torque. Quite frequently these patients will complain of either medial thigh pain or pes anserine insertional pain. Finally, the tibialis posterior will be challenged through all three phases of contraction, especially eccentrically, in an attempt to slow the pronation.

Forefoot valgus can be in compensation to a cavus foot. It will depend on the size of the deformity and rigidity/flexibility of the deformity. Rigid deformity has limited midtarsal and 1st ray motion, and results in supination of the subtalar joint. Flexible

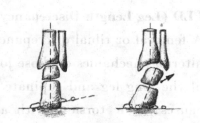

Forefoot valgus

deformity allows the forefoot to reach the ground via inversion of the forefoot along the midtarsal joint axis.

1st ray dorsiflexion/plantar flexion: The 1st ray is the medial cuneiform, 1st metatarsal and its associated phalanges. Movement abnormalities may result from congenital deformity, osseous or soft tissue restrictions which will alter its function. By holding the foot in neutral, the 1st ray will be lower than the other metatarsals (plantar flexed). Congenital plantar flexion will usually dorsiflex and plantar flex through equal ranges of motion. Acquired deformities are usually more rigid and will require greater compensation. The ability to compensate depends on the rigidity of the deformity and amount of subtalar pronation/supination available.

EVALUATION WHILE SUPINE

Motion palpation: What specific fixations do you find? A subluxated talonavicular joint can cause arch pain as well as slow or prevent normal pronation from occurring, as can other fixations. You can be fooled into a false forefoot/rear foot posture (ex. Valgus/varus) as well. Evaluate, manipulate, mobilize, reevaluate, BEFORE you cast or formulate an opinion.

LLD (Leg Length Discrepancy): Is the discrepancy femoral, tibial, or pelvic? A femoral or tibial discrepancy will change the axis of knee motion, further altering mechanics of those joints. A person will usually pronate on the side of the long leg and supinate on the side of the short leg LLD. This often causes pelvic torsion, with a flexion fixation on the long leg side and/or extension on the side of the LLD. Overpronation also causes excessive internal rotation of the thigh on that side, causing additional torque on the hip and SI joint, as well as tension/torsional stresses on the piriformis and external rotators (superior and inferior gemelli, obturator internus and externus, quadratus femoris). See also the LLD chapter for more information on LLD's.

Hip flexion (120°): Flexion less than 30° will mean problems with the leg clearing the ground during swing phase, and may result in toe drag, abducting the pelvis to the opposite side, circumducting the lower extremity, or contralateral ankle plantar flexion to elevate the pelvis for clearance of the toes. Often, flexion occurs within the lumbar spine (which can be damaging to the IVD, especially when combined with a torsional component, such as with a unilateral or asymmetrical pronation). An attempt to improve hip flexion can occur from several strategies but the most common is a compensated Trendelenberg gait. In this strategy the patient leans further than normal over the stance phase limb in an attempt to pull or carry the contralateral hip into adequate pelvic lift and thus adequate hip flexion to clear the limb. This pattern is met with contraction of the quadratus lumborum on the affected side, hip abductor (gluteus medius) contraction on the stance side, and possibly recruitment of the swing side abdominal and paraspinals (iliocostalis lumborum).

Knee Flexion (135°)/Knee Extension (0°): These ranges of motion will help to understand the shock absorbing ability of the leg as well as its behavior, at or near a closed pack position. When the knee is non-weight bearing, as in swing phase, extension causes internal femoral rotation (with a greater ROM at the medial condyle) and external tibial rotation. If the knee goes into a closed pack position, the popliteus must contract to "unlock" the knee, before it is able to flex. In a closed pack position, the thigh and leg behave as a single unit. The knee needs to be fully extended at heel strike to help decelerate the body and help initiate pronation and at heel lift to help with propulsion. Inadequate knee flexion at heel lift will mean that the motion will have to occur at the ankle.

Hip internal rotation (40°)/Hip external rotation (45°): This can be limited by

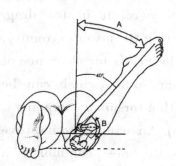

developmental (anteversion/retroversion), bony/cartilaginous, ligamentous or muscular factors. The femur must internally rotate approximately 4-5° by the end of terminal stance, and externally 4-6° by the end of toe off. If it is unable to go through this ROM, the motion must occur elsewhere (pelvis, ankle). *Also see prone evaluation.*

SLR (Straight Leg Raise) (90°): This is a measurement of hamstring/gluteal length, and also reflects the anatomical condition of the hip joint. Tight hamstrings often occur (along with tightening or shortening of the lumbar erectors or QL) in the presence of gluteal insufficiency due to reciprocal inhibition from the hip flexors. A decreased ROM and or increase in LBP or leg pain with internal rotation and decrease with ER often is caused by tight external rotators. Piriformis involvement is often implicated with sciatic pain (the sciatic nerve passes under the piriformis in 80% of people and through in 2-3%)

70

EVALUATION WHILE PRONE

Hip internal rotation (40°)/ Hip external rotation (45°): This may be a function of femoral anteversion/retroversion, acetabular anatomy, condition of the ilio/ishio/pubofemoral ligaments, or the surrounding hip musculature. The femur must internally rotate approximately 4-5° by the end of terminal stance, and externally 4-6° by the end of preswing. If it is unable to go through this ROM, the motion must occur elsewhere (pelvis, ankle).

Internal hip rotation through the midstance to heel rise phases of gait is critical for normal pronation and forefoot pressures. Without adequate internal hip rotation the patient will not be able to get over the medial aspect of the foot and pronate adequately. Instead, they will progress through midstance until they reach the internal rotation limit and then they will have to employ an alternate strategy to complete the heel rise and toe off phases. They will do this by adducting the heel (abducting / externally rotating the foot) and externally rotating the limb. This will cause a shift of the weight bearing away from the medial foot and onto the lesser metatarsals. Pronation will be minimized and replaced by a rolling off of the inside of the hallux.

Hip Extension (30°): Inadequate extension (<10°) will alter heel strike and heel lift phases of gait, often causing the motion to occur in the lumbar spine instead (in hyperextension). Again, there can be osseous, ligamentous and muscular reasons for this. If the hip flexors are tight, the gluteal muscles will be inhibited

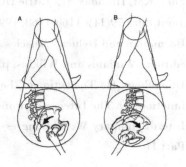

(through reciprocal inhibition), and the person will be forced to use the ipsilateral erectors and hamstrings to decelerate the leg at heel strike. The plantar flexors of the ankle can become chronically strained at heel lift, as they will be forced to go through a greater ROM.

References:
Hoppenfeld: Examination of the Spine and Extremities; Appleton Century Crofts, Norwalk, CT 1976
Rothstein, Roy, Wolf: The Rehabilitation Specialists Handbook; FA Davis, Philadelphia, PA 1991
Micahud: Foot Orthoses and Other Forms of Conservative Foot Care; 517 Washington Street, Newton MA 617-969-2225
Frankel, Nordin: Basic Biomechanics of the Skeletal System; Lea & Febiger, Philadelphia, PA 1980
Subotnick S. Case History of unilateral short leg with athletic overuse injury. JAPA 1980; 5: 255-256
Valmassey R. Clinical Biomechanics of the lower extremities. Mosby, St Louis, Philadelphia. 101-107: 1996
Shawn Eno, personal communication
Botte RR: An interpretation of the pronation syndrome and foot types of patients with low back pain. JAPA 71: 243-253, 1981
Blake RL, Fregeson HJ. Correlation between limb length discrepancy and assymetrical rearfoot position JAPA 83(11): 625-33, 1993
Song KM, Halliday SE, Little DG. The effect of limb length discrepancy on gait. J Bone Joint Surg 79(11): 1160-1168, 1997
Basmajian and Deluca. Muscles Alive: Their functions revealed by electromyography. 5th edition. Williams and Wilkins, p311, 1985
Dananberg, H. The action of the lower extremity and its relationship to lumbosacral function. In The Integrated Function of the Lumbar Spine and Sacroiliac Joint. Second Interdisciplinary World Congress on Low Back Pain. P 463-470. SanDiego Nov 9-11, 1995 Part II

Leg length discrepancies and heel lifts.
To lift or not to lift...

Leg length discrepancies (LLD's) are encountered on a daily basis. They are the root of many ankle, knee, hip and spinal problems. The questions the clinician must ask are "How much is significant?", "How much do I add?" What are some of the signs and symptoms?" "What is the etiology?" and "How do I detect it?"

How much is significant?

Most authorities claim that deficiencies of greater than ¼ inch (6mm) are clinically significant (1, 2) though some sources state that differences as little as 4 mm are significant (5). Subotnick (3) states that because of the threefold increase in ground reactive forces with running, lifts should be used with inequalities of greater than 1/8" inch (3mm).

How much do I add?

One of the easiest ways to determine the amount of lift needed is to examine the person in a weight bearing posture and add lifts under the short leg until the pelvis is even or until the lumbar spine is straight. If using off weight bearing measurements, you need to add 1/3 more height than measured because the talus is positioned 1/3 of the way between the calcaneus and metatarsal heads (4, 13). So, a heel lift placed under the calcaneus will only raise the talus 2/3 of that height. Lifts placed under the calcaneus can shorten the tricep surae muscles (4, 6) and apply increased pressure to the metatarsal heads (12); full length sole lifts are more physiological, though not always practical (A sole lift will raise the entire foot in the shoe which will equally elevate the heel and forefoot to the same plane. The problem that often

73

arises is that the shoe volume in the toe box is reduced and the patient can complain of the dorsum of the toes and toe nails contacting the roof of the shoe. One solution is to abbreviate the sole lift by cutting it short just distal to the metatarsal heads so that the toe box volume is not compromised. We have found that this rectifies the volume issue but on a rare occasion another problem can arise. In this case occasionally the patient can develop some flexor hallucis longus tenderness or toe flexor exertional achiness in the arch of the foot. This rarely occurs but when it does it is due to the increased distance that the toes have to move into flexion to contact the sole of the shoe from its newly lifted position. We have found that this can be mostly rectified by tapering the sole lift from the metatarsal head interval to the end of the sole lift. This gives a more gradual tapering and allows the full sole lift to be used without compromising too much toe box volume.

Due to the supinatory moment of the short leg on heel strike, a lift may cause overcompensation and increased supination, with a tendency to overweight the lateral column and possibly injure the lateral ankle. Careful observation of gait post addition of a lift is in order and a valgus post running at least the length of the 5th metatarsal along with the lift should be considered (8, 9). Heel lifts also cause EMG changes of leg muscles, with decreased recruitment of gastrocnemius and tibialis anterior directly proportional to the height of the heel lift (18, 19). A lift or LLD changes the ground reactive forces associated with gait, increasing vertical force on the longer leg, along with increased joint stresses along the kinetic chain (14, 20).

Generally speaking, lifts greater than 3/8" (9mm) require extrinsic modifications to footwear (4, 6, 8). Find a competent individual to perform this work for you. Large discrepancies should be treated gradually, at a rate of ¼ inch every 4 weeks, less if symptoms do not permit.

What are signs and symptoms associated with LLD's?

Compensation comes in many forms, depending whether it is acute (recent injury caused an LLD or compensation resulting in one, or long term. The deficiency can cause injury on the short or long legged side (or both). It is our opinion that the signs and symptoms of LLD are patient specific and even that which appears as a trivial amount may be the source of pain or symptoms at the foot or far reaching depending on activity, sustained postures and duration of time that the pathology has been building. It is critical to keep in mind that the patient's complaints may be an indirect result of muscular compensations or joint mechanics compensations that have developed as a result of the LLD. Quite often these complaints may not make sense in regards to an LLD but may be an indirect result thereof as the body compensates elsewhere in an attempt to either rectify the LLD or to put into place measures to reduce the impact of those forces on a particular joint.

The long leg moves through a greater arc during all portions of swing phase (7). The person may flex the knee to compensate and shorten the arc. The individual may also maximally pronate and evert the calcaneus an additional 3 degrees or greater on that side in an attempt to lower the navicular to the ground and shorten that leg. This causes an increased amount of internal rotation of the tibia and thigh causing muscular dysfunction (tightness of the hip flexors, strain of the intrinsic external rotators from eccentric deceleration of the thigh), along with medial knee strain (especially with concomitant genu valgus) (4, 6, 8, 9, 10, 11, 21, 22, 23).

Blustein and D'Amico (23) state that short leg side will often supinate in an attempt to lengthen and cushion some of the shock of heel strike. This contradicts the findings of Sobotnick (24, 25) who states most people externally rotate the short limb, causing excessive pronation. Bloedel and Hauger (26) found no significant differences between calcaneal inversion and eversion ranges of motion in individuals with limb length discrepancies of ½ - 3/4 inches, suggesting that subtalar mechanics were not significantly altered.

Liu et al (27) state that the majority of the compensations from a LLD are in the pelvis, hip and knee. From their study, it was clear that a number of compensatory mechanisms play a role in the gait of patients with LLD. They state that the mechanism of compensation depends on the amount of LLD. As long as the difference remains below a mean of 2.64 cm, the compensation is located in the pelvis, hip and knee joints. Flexion in the hip joint at heel strike is augmented on the long side, while it is reduced in the short leg at midstance and toe-off, in combination with increased knee flexion at heel strike. Both of these mechanisms aim to minimize pelvic tilt. Meanwhile, this reduced hip flexion and functional lengthening of the short leg provide necessary clearance for the contralateral (long) leg to swing through.

According to Liu once the leg length discrepancy reaches about 4 cm, the aforementioned compensations in the pelvis, hip and knee joints diminish and the ankle joint compensates. Dorsiflexion during midstance is appreciably diminished, while plantar flexion at toe-off is dramatically increased. This again results in a functional lengthening of the short leg allowing for clearance of the long leg. Using a heel lift to correct inequality to a mean LLD of 5 mm results in a reduction of knee flexion in the long leg, producing a relative functional shortening of that leg. Using a heel lift that leaves a mean LLD of about 1.4 cm, the functional shortening of the long leg during stance still exists, but at different periods of stance phase. However, believed that the heel lift did not affect the pelvis, the hip joint, or the ankle joint, which may mean the heel lift causes a forward inclination of the body and easily moves forward a vertical ground reaction force in front of the knee to reduce the flexion moment. We tend to concur with Liu in that from the changes in kinematics, it is impossible to decide on the ideal acceptable amount of leg-length discrepancy (LLD) because patients will demonstrate significant biomechanical effects on different joints in attempts to reach symmetric gait patterning. As a result of symmetric gait patterns, the hip joint on the long side provides more flexion, the knee joint on the short side increases extension, and the ankle joint on the short side increases plantar flexion as discussed previously.

Since the short leg has a greater vertical distance to travel (14); this often causes hyperextension of that knee. This lessens the dampening ability of the knee (since it flexes almost 20 degrees between heel strike and full forefoot load), and speeds the rate of subtalar pronation (since the rear foot is inverted and still must pronate the same amount (4). Many individuals will try and attenuate impact by contracting the contralateral hip abductor muscles and eccentrically lower the shorter extremity (4, 14). This can produce excessive strain of that musculature (trochanteric bursitis, ilio tibial band functional shortening and quite possibly length-tension adjustments to the contralateral biceps femoris) as well as pathomechanical abnormalities of the L4 and L5 motion segments (due to increased body rotation toward the short side and attachments of the iliolumbar ligaments; this can cause degenerative changes if present long term (11, 12).

These rotational compensations will frequently generate a clockwise or counterclockwise pelvic distortion pattern which creates a whole host of compensations in the proximal limb and pelvis. Hip capsular patterns of tightness will develop most frequently in the posterior capsule of the short limb side due to the counter nutation-like or extension movement of the same side hemi pelvis (upper hemi pelvis posterior rotation, lower hemi pelvis anterior rotation) in an attempt to lengthen the limb. This compensation will reduce adequate and efficient posterior femoral head glide and rotation into the posterior acetabulum and thus not challenge the posterior hip capsule to maintain its normal length. This phenomenon can be seen quite easily if the patient is asked to stand in front of the examiner and bend forward at the waist. As the patient bends forward the pelvis can be seen to rotate away from the short leg-tight posterior hip capsule as flexion progresses (i.e. If the left leg is found short, the left hemi pelvis will rotate posteriorly and the left hip capsule will be posteriorly tight. As the patient flexes forward, the pelvis will begin rotating in a clockwise fashion as the tight posterior hip capsule is engaged.)

As mentioned above these compensations will easily impact normal force transfer into the spine and impact lumbar motion segment function. It is also quite common to see a frontal plane shift to the side of the short limb. This means that the attempt to normalize the short leg length is not sufficient. Thus, the patient will not only drop the pelvis lower on the short leg side to reach the ground but the momentum will carry the pelvis a greater distance to that side. This will necessitate the recruitment of the short side hip abductors (gluteus medius, ilio tibial band, tensor fascial lata and even the ipsilateral quadratus lumborum) to slow the excessive lateral movement of the pelvis and torso over the short leg. This recruitment will be of the eccentric variety and may generate the following undesirable compensations: short leg side stretch-weakness of the abductor group and tightness of the adductors with the opposite reaction on the longer leg side, those being abductor shortness and stretch-weakness of the adductors. Keep in mind that the compensations will not remain isolated in these frontal plane muscle groups, there will be great spill over into the surrounding muscles as the body attempts to control the rotational components imparted on the hip, pelvis, knee, and lower limb.

Long leg adaptations	Short leg adaptations
• Drooping of shoulder with elevation of iliac crest on long leg side	• raised shoulder with depression of iliac crest on long leg side
• Piriformis/external rotator tightness	• TFL tightness
• Tightness of hip flexors	• Decreased lordosis
• Increased lordosis	• Anterior rotation (extension) of the ilia (can lengthen leg up to 6mm)
• Posterior rotation (flexion) of ilia (can shorten leg up to 6mm	• Lateral knee degenerative changes
• Medial knee degenerative changes/pain	• Increased supination?

What's the etiology?

LLD's can be structural (anatomical) or functional (pathomechanics, compensation). LLD's can be due to foot problems (overpronation/supination, fractures), leg or thigh problems (congenital shortening, deformity, fracture), or pelvic compensation (rotation of ilia, fractures).

So, what *is* the etiology? A lot can be gleaned from the history. Past trauma is the most obvious so pay close attention. This could result in flattening of the calcaneus or overpronation due to ligamentous laxity; tibial fractures can cause shortening as well as increased or decreased tibial torsion; similar findings can occur in the femur, along with anteversion or retroversion; pelvic trauma can be more subtle and x-ray can often provide the most information (1, 2, 4, 6).

As we have alluded to already, one of the more proximal causes of LLD is from pelvis and hip compensations. Hip flexion while standing erect can be present due to weakness or excessive length (stretch-weakness) of the external oblique or rectus abdominis muscle; their weakness allows the anterior rim of the pelvis (ASIS) to drop thus forcing flexion at the hip. This may lead to a same side sway back phenomenon which can lead to a very complex biomechanical phenomenon known as femoral glide syndrome. Any patient with unilateral hip or pelvic pain will have abdominal wall dysfunction as evidenced by tenderness, increased tone and myofascial dysfunction in the wall. We frequently find the tenderness and myofascial points on the contralateral side but there may be ipsilateral compensation as well. Normal hip flexor length and adequate performance of the abdominal muscles to control pelvic tilt is critical in controlling lumbar spine lordosis.

The same can be said for controlling posterior pelvic tilting. However, when the hip flexor muscles are short in relation to the abdominal muscles (synergistic pair), instead of the compensation being reflected in hip motion, there may be exaggerated anterior pelvic tilt and increased lumbar extension. A simple rule of thumb should be to look at the length-tension relationships of the single and multi-joint muscles about the hip and pelvis. Any aberration will result in abnormal positioning, function and leg length. Thus, without adequate abdominal core strength, length, synchrony and timely activation, the hip biomechanics can be compromised leading to a proximal-to-distal kinetic chain breakdown and thus a possible leg length discrepancy.

There is one more perspective that should be entertained, that being a distal injury such ankle inversion-eversion events causing an LLD or the LLD being the cause of the injury. In the LLD patient the hip on the high iliac crest side is in adduction and the contralateral hip is in abduction (see diagram). The problem may be weakness or insufficiency of the hip abductor muscles. The hip abduction on one side and adduction on the other can lead to the occurrence of ankle sprains. The ankle may be affected by an apparent LLD in two ways. Usually on the side of the adducted hip (high iliac crest), the functionally short leg side, the foot will be supinated (the right foot in the diagram). During running or rapid changes in direction as in sports, excessive length or weakness (stretch-weakness is also possible) of the hip abductor muscles will allow the hip to move too far laterally in the frontal plane (in this case to the right) over the foot when the foot is on the ground or allow the hip to adduct excessively during the swing phase of gait. The

excessive hip adduction in both situations and the supinated position of the foot can contribute to inversion injuries of the ankle. The problem arises since the line of gravity is shifted medial to the hip and lateral to the ankle. Therefore, a comprehensive therapy program for the inversion injury patient or for the short leg patient should include hip abductor exercises, primarily focusing on the closed kinetic chain.

How do you determine a leg length inequality?

There are a number of methods, each with their own merit. X —ray is most accurate, but exposes the patient to ionizing radiation. Weight bearing seems most appropriate, since symptomatology usually presents itself then. Supine measurements are said to be influenced by asymmetrical muscle tension, table pressure on the innominates and hip flexor length (15).

With the patient weight bearing and both feet placed below the trochanters, observe the level of the medial malleoli. Next, compare the heights of the tibial plateaus. Femoral length can be judged by the heights of the greater trochanters, and pelvic alignment judged by the heights of the iliac crests (4, 17).

Alternately, lay the person supine and observe the heels and medial malleoli. If there is noticeable discrepancy, they may have a short leg; if there isn't, they still may have a discrepancy that they are compensating for. Check the range of motion of the foot and ankle in 6 general directions: plantar flexion (40-45 degrees), dorsiflexion (20-25 degrees, depending on whether the knee is flexed or extended), inversion of the forefoot (3-60 degrees, on average), and eversion of the forefoot (20-45 degrees on average), calcaneal inversion (4-20 degrees) and calcaneal eversion (4-10 degrees). Excessive calcaneal eversion usually means over pronation due to a longer leg on that side; excessive inversion can mean a long leg due to a cavus foot type (2, 4, 6, 8, 9, 12). Lack of flexibility in the posterior compartment of the calf usually causes a greater degree of pronation (16).

Now, perform Allis's test. Bend both knees to 90 degrees and observe the height of the tibial plateaus. The lower one is usually the side of the

82

discrepancy (which can be in tibial length, subtalar anatomy, calcaneal anatomy or due to excessive pronation). Now walk superior to the knees and observe the femurs from more cephalad (4). Is there a discrepancy? If so, the problem may be in the femur length, femoral head angle or pelvis. Extend the knees so that the legs are lying flat on the exam table. Palpate the greater trochanters on both sides. Is one lower than the other? If so, they probably have coxa vara on the short side or coxa valga on the long side. If they are even, you need to look at the pelvis. Does one ASIS palpate more anterior or posterior than the other? This could represent compensation. A posterior or "flexed" ilia, usually causes a short leg on that side; an anterior or extended ilia usually causes a long leg on that side.

Now stand the patient up and perform a Gillet Test. Have them stand erect and hold onto something for balance. Palpate the PSIS on one side along with the 2nd sacral tubercle. Have them raise their thigh to 90 degrees on the side you are palpating. The PSIS should nutate backward (flex) and drop .5-1.5 cm on the side of the raised leg. Now have them raise the opposite leg. The sacrum should nutate backward and down. If either of these movements does not occur, consider pelvic pathomechanics and treat accordingly. Recheck for motion as well as leg length when done.

Standing observation often (but not always) reveals overpronation on the long leg side and relative supination on the short leg side. The shoulder is often higher on the short side and the waistline dips to the long side because of posterior rotation of the innominate. The shoulder will dip to the side of the short leg on heel strike during dynamic evaluation (4, 6, 8, 9, 10, 11). Gait observation usually reveals adduction of the pelvis toward the stance phase leg with a lateral sway in excess of 1" during stance phase. The person will seem like they are "stepping into a hole" on the short side.

Conclusion

Leg length inequalities occur due to a variety of anatomical and physiological conditions. Careful analysis and examination can often reveal its etiology. To lift or not to lift is a clinical decision that is left to the clinician and patient, with a careful balance between what is perceived as improved biomechanics and tolerance levels of the patient with regards to their presenting symptomatology.

References
1 Cyriax J. Textbook of Orthopedic Medicine Vol I, 5th Ed. London: Baillare, Tyndall and Cassell, 1969
2 Taillard W. Lumbar Spine and Leg Length Inequality. Acta Orthop Belg 1969; 35: 601
3 Subotnick S. Case History of unilateral short leg with athletic overuse injury. JAPA 1980; 5: 255-256
4 Micahud T. Foot Orthoses and other forms of conservative foot care. Newton, MA 114-117: 1993
5 Martens M, Backaert M, et al. Chronic leg pain in athletes due to a recurrent compartment syndrome. Am J Sports Med 12: 148-151: 1984
6 Valmassey R. Clinical Biomechanics of the lower extremities. Mosby, St Louis, Philadelphia. 101-107: 1996
7 Press SJ. A report of clinical applications of computers in analysis of gait spinal imbalances. Chiro Sports Med 1987;1:30
8 Shawn Eno, personal communication
9 personal observation
10 Botte RR: An interpretation of the pronation syndrome and foot types of patients with low back pain. JAPA 71: 243-253, 1981

11 Friberg O: Clinical symptoms and biomechanics of lumbar spine and hip joint in leg length inequality. Spine 8: 643-651, 1983

12 Rothenberg RJ: Rheumatic disease aspects of leg length inequality. Sem Arth Rheum 17: 196-205, 1988

13 Travell J, Simons D. Myofascial Pain and Dysfunction: The Trigger Point Manual. Baltimore: Williams and Wilkins 112, 1983

14 Schuit D, Adrian M, Pidcoe P. Effects of heel lifts on ground reactive force patterns in subjects with structural leg length discrepancies. Phys Ther 69(8): 41-48, 1989

15 Rothbart BA, Estabrook L. Excessive Pronation: a Major biomechanical determinant in the development of chondromalacia and pelvic lists. JMPT 5: 373-379, 1988

16 Kirby KA Effect of Heel Height Differential in Shoes on Orthosis Function. Precision Intracast Newsletter, March 1987, 1-3

17 Hoffmn KS, Hoffman LL. Effects of adding sacral base leveling to osteopathic manipulative treatment of back pain: A pilot study JAOA 94 (3): 217-220, 223-226 1994

18 Lee KH, Shieh JC, et al. Electromyographic changes of leg muscles with heel lifts in women: therapeutic implications. Arch Phys Med Rehabil 71(1): 31-3, 1990

19 Lee KH, Matteliano A, et al. Electromyographic changes of leg muscles with heel lift: therapeutic implications Arch Phys Med Rehabil 68(5 pt 1): 298-301, 1987

20 McCrory JL, White SC, Lifeso RM: Vertical ground reaction forces: objective measures of gait following hip arthroplasty Gait Posture 14(2): 104-109, 2001

21 Blake RL, Fregeson HJ. Correlation between limb length discrepancy and assymetrical rearfoot position JAPA 83(11): 625-33, 1993

22 Song KM, Halliday SE, Little DG. The effect of limb length discrepancy on gait. J Bone Joint Surg 79(11): 1160-1168, 1997

23 Blustein SM, D'Amico JC. Limb length discrepancy: Identification, clinical significance and management. JAPA 75(4) 200-206, 1985

24 Subotnick SI. The biomechanics of running implications for the prevention of foot injuries. Sports Med 2: 144-153, 1985

25 Subotnick SI. Limb length discrepancies of the lower extremity (the short leg syndrome). JOSPT 3(1): 11-16, 1981

26 Bloedel P, Hauger B. The effects of limb length discrepancy on subtalar joint kinematics during running. JOSPT 22(2): 60-64, 1995

27 Liu X. C. , Thometz J., Fabry G, Molenaers G, Lammens J, Moens P. Function Analysis: Leg length discrepancy defines gait patterns. Decisions about treatment or interventions for people with LLD can be influenced by compensation mechanisms.BioMechanics,December1998

Pedograph Analysis

Having a reasonable understanding of the gait cycle, you are now ready to approach pedograph analysis in a logical, consistent manner. Remember it is a 2 dimensional snapshot of one moment in time during the gait cycle. It merely tells you where there are increased or decreased plantar pressures. You must interpret the results in light of what you see during static and dynamic evaluation of the foot. Please remember that the information obtained from your pedograph is only as good as your pedograph technique. Please be sure to obey all of the rules and techniques we have put forth here in this manual. We have learned from experience what works and what gives false impressions and thus false reads. Sloppy technique and set up will give pedograph readings that may conflict with your clinical impressions and examination. This is why we will constantly remind you to pay most attention to your clinical examination and history, at least until you develop a solid and reproducible pedograph mapping technique. Remember, the patient produces the impression, it is up to you to set them up correctly and educate them in what to do and what not to do to ensure the best mapping possible.

The pedograph measures pressure gradients. More ink = more little grid marks = more pressure. Calluses, bony protruberances, prominent ends of bone (met heads, fallen naviculars, etc), even dirt and sand will all leave a greater impression. Often times an area of increased pressure is artifact (schmutz on the foot or on or under the rubber canopy), so careful inspection is in order!

For our intents and purposes, the foot (and thus the pedograph) can be divided into 3 areas: rearfoot, midfoot and forefoot. We will examine each area systematically following what should be the normal transmission of forces through the foot. Note the overall impression, medial and lateral borders, and anterior/ posterior dimensions. In each of the proceeding sections, pay close attention to the area of the foot being discussed, as this is the area of the pedograph being discussed. There will often be abnormalities in other areas as well, which are discussed in other sections.

Rearfoot

The rearfoot consists of the calcaneus and talus. It will be influenced by the available motions at this articulation, superincumbent forces from above as the body's weight is imparted on them, as well as at the talo-navicular and calcaneocuboid joints.

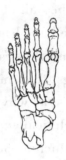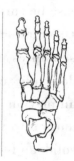

We have identified 6 predominant rearfoot patterns (which can occur in various combinations) as follows:

Normal motion
Heavier/lighter heel strike
Rearfoot pronation (excess calcaneal eversion, calcaneal valgus)
Rearfoot supination (rearfoot varus)
Fat pad displacement
Motion artifact

Normal motion: symmetrical weight distribution from side to side (same number of gridlines).

Appearance: The imprint has a rounded, teardrop shape with a triangular departure at the anterior lateral aspect and a rounded medial departure antero-medially.

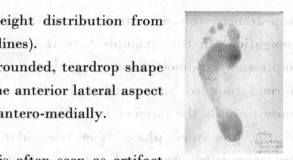

Heavier/lighter heel strike: this is often seen as artifact

from printing (the person steps further or heavier) on one side. It is also seen on the side of the longer leg or in people with a rigid, cavus midfoot with little shock attenuation.

Appearance: increased ink or number of gridlines under heel.

Note increased pressure laterally and medially with some anterior smudging

Excessive rearfoot pronation: Remember that the calcaneus should evert after initial contact and should continue to do so until midstance. The amount of eversion will be limited by the amount of available eversion. This pathology is present with calcaneal valgus and increased available calcaneal eversion. It is often accompanied by increased midfoot pronation and occasionally by a rigid forefoot varus (the calcaneus continues to roll medially after full eversion). An aggressive tibial varum will accentuate or maximize any available calcaneal eversion (see explanation under Tibal Varum), though this deformity will often present with a rigid rear and midfoot.

Appearance: widened anterior, medial border with elongation. In this example here the darker heel impression is almost boomerang shaped with the normal rounded anteromedial departure dragged more towards the forefoot indicating a prolonging of the pronatory phase. The triangular lateral departure is less acute and distinct indicating that the normal progression forces have been shifted medially instead of progressing distally into the forefoot. In severe cases, the imprint extends into the midfoot and the navicular imprint is seen.

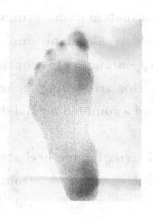

Rearfoot supination: This is caused by inadequate calcaneal eversion or a fixed rearfoot varus.

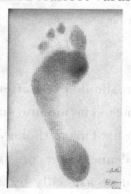

Appearance: increased lateral pressure with a shortened anterior medial imprint which is often less rounded. The imprint is elongated anterolaterally with a more acute triangular departure.

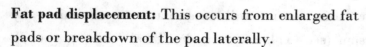

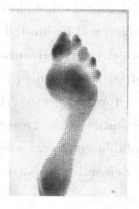

Fat pad displacement: This occurs from enlarged fat pads or breakdown of the pad laterally.

Appearance: increased splay of heel with elongation laterally and longitudinally. There is often a "halo" effect with less pressure laterally and more medially (from the calcaneal tuberosity)

Motion artifact: This happens when the heel slides on the rubber canopy. It occurs when the patient's initial positioning is too far from the pedographs leading edge. This can also occur from a pant cuff or sock fold or from the pedograph sliding on the floor.

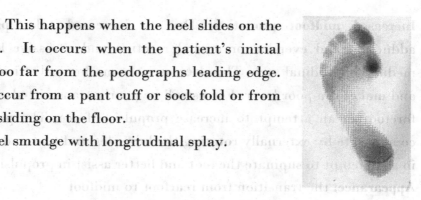

Appearance: heel smudge with longitudinal splay.

Midfoot

The midfoot consists of the talonavicular, calcaneocuboid, cuneiform-metatarsal and cuboid-metatarsal articulations. It will be influenced by available motion in both the rearfoot and forefoot.

We have identified 3 predominant midfoot patterns as follows:

Normal
Increased midfoot pronation
Decreased midfoot pronation (relative supination)

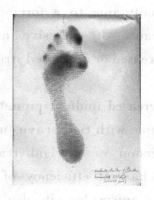

Normal: the width has bilateral symmetry with an hourglass shape.
Appearance: There is a slight triangular transition from the rearfoot to midfoot which becomes an inverted triangle as they pass through midstance.

Pressures show a slight preponderance laterally, as forces travel up the lateral column. This signifies an adequate calcaneocuboid locking mechanism.

Increased midfoot pronation: Due to increased talar plantar flexion, adduction and eversion or medial rotation and excessive lowering of the medial longitudinal arch. This decreases the mechanical efficiency of the foot and makes it a poor lever. Forces will be poorly transmitted anteriorly to the forefoot in an attempt to increase propulsive force. The person will often compensate by externally rotating the lower leg and foot and firing the FHL in an attempt to supinate the foot and better assist in propulsion.

Appearance: the transition from rearfoot to midfoot is indistinct and the medial and lateral borders are nearly parallel. As midfoot pronation increases, the anterior medial aspect of the teardrop becomes indistinct ad sometimes squared. The entire medial longitudinal arch can become obliterated. The notch formed by the styloid can become more (in a person with a more mobile midfoot and rearfoot, usually due to a forefoot varus) or less distinct because of excessive midfoot eversion due to increased or decreased structure and relative foot rigidity.

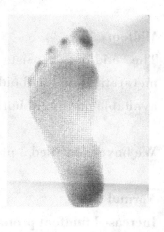

Decreased midfoot pronation (or relative supination): This is often seen in people with rigid, cavus midfeet. It is often accompanied by limited rearfoot eversion or a rigid rearfoot varus deformity. It represents increased mechanical efficiency of the lateral column and calcaneocuboid locking mechanism but it also represents poor adaptive and shock absorptive pronatory capabilities. It often occurs on the side of a functional or anatomical short leg; in an attempt to lengthen the extremity (supination raises the relative positional height of the talus).

Appearance: The hourglass shape is accentuated and sometimes interrupted. The imprint of the styloid process of the 5th metatarsal is often seen depending on the height of the lateral longitudinal arch. The person often attempts to compensate in the forefoot.

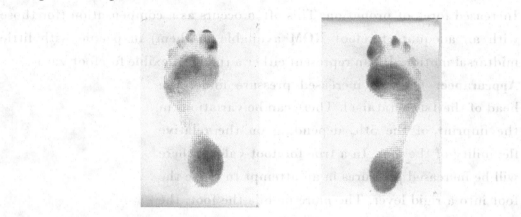

Forefoot

The forefoot consists of the distal metatarsal heads and phalanges. It will reflect the amount of available motion in the midfoot.

We have identified 4 predominant patterns:

Normal
Increased forefoot pronation (eversion)
Decreased forefoot pronation (inversion or supination)
Plantar flexed 1st (rigid, compensated forefoot varus)

Normal: There is increased pressure in the center of the 1st metatarsal head and distal phalynx of the great toe. The imprints of the lesser toes are all visible and symmetrical. You can expect to see printing under the flexor hallicus longus tendon at its insertion point at the distal hallux. There can also be slight increased pressure under the head of the 5th metatarsal (due to the tripod formed by the calcaneus, head of 1st and head of 5th.

Increased forefoot pronation: This often occurs as a compensation (for those with an adequate forefoot ROM available to them) in people with little midtarsal motion. It can represent either a rigid or flexible forefoot varus.

Appearance: There is increased pressure under the head of the 1st metatarsal. There can be variations in the imprint of the 5th, depending on the relative flexibility of the foot. In a true forefoot valgus, there will be increased pressures in an attempt to make the foot into a rigid lever. The more mobile the foot, the more pressure will be under the 2nd and 3rd metatarsal heads with less relative pressure under the 1st and 5th metatarsal heads. This occurs in part 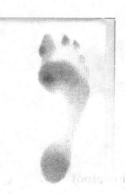 because as the 1st metatarsal dorsiflexes in hyperpronation it elevates as does the 5th metatarsal. This changes the tension on the transverse metatarsal ligament thus increasing the relative plantar pressure under the middle three met heads. This scenario is one which leads to eventual bunion and hallux valgus development as the anchor to the adductor hallucis muscle is lost.

Decreased forefoot pronation: This is typically seen in an uncompensated forefoot varus, where there is limited forefoot ROM in eversion available.

94

Appearance: there is less pressure under the 1st and increased pressure under

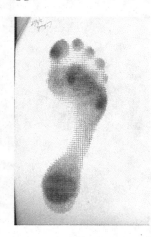

the 2nd, 3rd and 4th met heads. You can occasionally see pressure under the medial aspect insertion of the FHL (at the distal IP joint) as they try to gain purchase to propel themselves forward. Depending on the age of the patient and the structure of the lateral column, you may see heavy pressure under the phalanges of 2-5 (increased flexor digitorum activation) to "claw" and gain mechanical advantage.

Plantar flexed 1st ray deformity: With this deformity, the 1st metatarsal head strikes the ground prematurely. It can be a flexible or rigid deformity. Root (1) called a congenital plantar flexed 1st the "most common cause of subtalar supination" and relates it to the development of a cavus foot type. It is often associated with a forefoot valgus deformity. Michaud (1) suggests that this is the end result or compensation for an inverted rigid rearfoot and midfoot, others state that it is a form of rigid forefoot valgus (a flexible forefoot valgus foot classically has little structure, and little ability to act as a rigid lever.

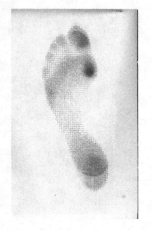

Appearance: There is greatly increased pressure under the head of the 1st metatarsal. There is zero ROM in calcaneal eversion and little midtarsal motion. Depending on the relative amount of plantar flexion of the 1st relative to the 5th, there will be little evidence of the distal phalynx imprint of the 5th and sometimes 4th. The styloid will rarely print.

References:
1. Root MC, Orion WP, Weed JH. Normal and Abnormal function of the foot. Los Angeles: Clinical Biomechanics, 1977
2. Michaud: Foot Orthoses and Other Forms of Conservative Foot Care; 517 Washington Street, Newton MA 617-969-2225

Case Studies

These are some of our actual cases with accompanying pedographs and clinical commentary provided for educational purposes. *Remember, there is often more than one explanation for what you are seeing.* **Always interpret your results in light of your examination findings.**

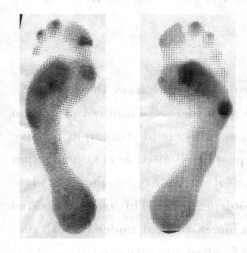

51 YO male with mild b/l external tibial torsion and genu varum on right. *He is having moderate to severe piriformis irritation on the right and mild on the left.*

There is moderate palpable IT band irritation on the right and mild on the left. There is posterior rotation of the pelvis on the right, anterior on the left. He has mild bunions b/l with some curling and hammering of the 5th digit on the right small toe. He has a Morton's foot, R > L. Ankle dorsiflexion is hypo mobile on the left. Calcaneal eversion is limited bilaterally, R > L. The midfoot is hypo mobile bilaterally. The forefoot is hypo mobile in eversion bilaterally and he has a forefoot varus. The 1st MPJ has adequate dorsi and plantarflexion. There is a 2 mm, right sided LLD. Gait reveals moderate forefoot abduction bilaterally with a varus calcaneus and mild external rotation of the knees.

Comments:

There is increased posterior and medial heel pressure on the left. There is increased midfoot pronation on the right. Pressure is markedly increased at the 5th metatarsal head on the right with incomplete forefoot pronation with pressure only extending to the 2nd metatarsal head. The left foot shows pressure over the 5th metatarsal head, then over 4, 3, 2 and finally 1, with increased heat under the distal phalynx of the great toe. No impression is seen from the distal phalynx of the 5th.

Discussion:

The increased heel pressure on the left probably stems from the LLD, and increased force at heel strike. You would expect increased midfoot pronation on this side as well, but that is not the case. This could stem from relative hypo mobility of the midtarsal joint and possibly limited ankle dorsiflexion on the left, which explains the diminished pronatory moment at late midstance to heel rise and increased forefoot pressures. This is compensated for by employing the FHL at toe off. The increased heat under the 5th met head (on the right) along with incomplete forefoot pronation on the right is consistent with a short leg on this side. This is probably exacerbated by the genu varum and short leg, both moving the center of gravity to the right. The bunion presentation bilaterally is expected when seeing this type of pedograph presentation because the increased 2-5 metatarsal head pressures and reduced 1st metatarsal pressures; thus the abductor hallucis will reverse its normal function. Rather than the 1st metatarsal acting as the anchor with the lesser metatarsals pulled towards it, the lesser metatarsals are better anchored and thus pull the hallux towards their stable origin.

98

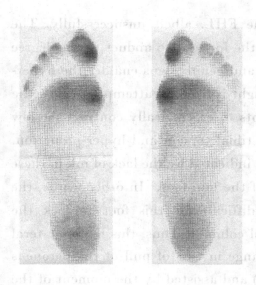

32 YO male with posterior tibialis tendonitis and peripatellar pain.

He has bilateral mild internal tibial torsion. There was mild piriformis pain on the right. There is a b/l forefoot varus deformity. The 1st ray has mild deviation to valgus. He has excessive calcaneal eversion and mid- tarsal motion. He has a short left leg by 5 mm Gait revealed excessive midfoot pronation with a genu valgus at the knee and adduction of the forefoot on toe off (inversion).

Comments:

There is increased heel pressure on the right and some bilateral splaying of the calcaneal fat pad. There is blunting of the medial aspect of the calcaneal teardrop bilaterally, R > L. The tail of the 5th metatarsal is visible on the right. Excessive midfoot pronation is seen bilaterally, R > L. Abduction of the forefoot is seen on the right proximal to the midtarsal joint. Little lateral and excessive medial forefoot pressures are noted, with heat under the distal 1st and great toe.

Discussion:

This is a case of a severe over pronator with a significant LLD. The increased heel pressure is consistent with the longer leg, as is the excessive midfoot pronation, R > L. The tail of the 5th metatarsal is visible as forefoot abduction occurs as the patient tries to create a rigid lever through midstance for toe off. He recruits the help of the FHL, albeit unsuccessfully. The excessive mid-tarsal mobility allows for the forefoot to abduct to the degree shown here. The internal tibial torsion and genu valgus enables the hyper-pronation. The piriformis pain on the right is from its attempts to slow the rate of internal limb rotation (it attempts to eccentrically contract to slow the rotation), a product of the internal tibial torsion and hyper-pronation. The reduced lateral forefoot pressures, as indicated by the lack of ink in these areas, confirms the increased mobility of the mid-foot. In other words, the increased mobility has made it very difficult for this foot to lock the calcaneocuboid joint and thus the lateral column. Thus, this mobile lateral column is free to abduct due to the change in axis of pull of the peroneus longus (pulls laterally rather than down) and assisted by the moment of the peroneus brevis and lateral extensor digitorum contract dragging the foot into abduction and further promoting the medial foot pressure predominance (hyperpronation). The increased pronation will place increased demands on the tibialis posterior, excessive eccentric demands, hence the pain in this tendon complex.

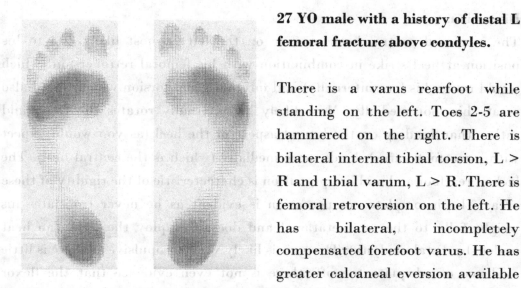

27 YO male with a history of distal L femoral fracture above condyles.

There is a varus rearfoot while standing on the left. Toes 2-5 are hammered on the right. There is bilateral internal tibial torsion, L > R and tibial varum, L > R. There is femoral retroversion on the left. He has bilateral, incompletely compensated forefoot varus. He has greater calcaneal eversion available on the left with relative hypo mobility in the rearfoot and midfoot with mild hypo mobility in the forefoot. He has a left short leg 3mm which is femoral. Gait evaluation reveals heel strike in inversion and abduction of the left leg through midswing. Moderate forefoot pronation is noted from late midstance through toe off.

Comments:
There is increased heel pressure centrally on the left with less midfoot pronation as he proceeds to midstance. There is increased pressure over the head of the 5th metatarsal bilaterally right slightly greater than the left, with increased plantar pressures over the 4th, 3rd and 2nd metatarsals bilaterally. There is slightly greater pressure over the 1st metatarsal on the right (compared to left).

Discussion:

The increased central heel pressure on the left is most likely due to his position at heel strike in combination with his femoral retroversion (which would rotate his foot internally) and internal tibial torsion which would also rotate his foot medially. Most likely he externally rotates the thigh and rather than landing on the lateral aspect of the heel (as you would expect with a rearfoot varus), lands more medially (which is the central heel). The lack of rearfoot and midfoot pronation is characteristic of the rigidity of these areas. His incomplete compensation is evident as he never translates his weight fully to the 1st metatarsal and doesn't employ the FHL (no heat under the distal phalynx). This gait is likely very apropulsive as there is little evidence of adequate toe off, there is not even evidence that the flexor digitorum is actively increased in function (no ink increase at the digits) although the clinical examination revealed digit hammering which is functionally confirmatory. The presence of the internal tibial torsion may have something to do with the lack of first met and FHL ink heat. The patient is possibly toeing off laterally to avoid the first ray complex toe off to avoid the added aggressive pronation that would occur if the first ray were engaged. Also, the suspect external thigh rotation will disengage some of the detrimental effects of the internal tibial torsion and improve the foot progression angle. Without the thigh external rotation the tibial torsion will promote a strong negative foot progression angle (pigeon toed) and hyperpronation.

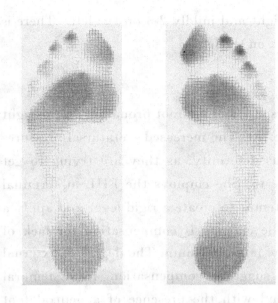

35 YO female.

There is moderate bilateral external tibial torsion with a mild genu valgum. The calcaneus is in mild valgus with weight bearing. She carries her right ASIS anterior in the gravitational plane. There are mild hallux abducto valgus deformities bilaterally and she has mild bilateral Morton's toes.

Calcaneal eversion is limited to approximately 4 degrees. The midfoot was hypo mobile and eversion was limited in the forefoot. She had bilateral rigid forefoot varus and 1st ray motion was limited in plantarflexion. She has a 3mm short leg (tibial) on the left. Gait evaluation revealed moderate midtarsal pronation during midstance and terminal stance. She had mild forefoot adduction at terminal stance to toe off. There was moderate internal rotation of the knee from midstance to toe off on the right and mildly so on the left. Her feet faced forward (creating more internal rotation of the knee) while walking.

Comments:

Heel pressure is increased on the right, with some splaying of the fat pad posteriorly and medially. There is more midfoot pronation on the right. There is increased pressure over metatarsal heads 2-4 bilaterally. There is slightly increased heat at the medial distal phalanyx of the 1st and evidence

103

of moderate clawing of 2-4 on the right and mildly 2-3 on the left. There is minimal printing of the 5th phalanyx on the left.

Discussion:

The increased heel pressure, fat pad splay and midfoot pronation on the right correlates well with the LLD on the left. The increased metatarsal pressures are consistent with a forefoot varus deformity, as they are trying to get weight over the 1st, but are unable to. She employs the FHL at terminal stance and heel rise/toe off in an attempt to create a rigid lever and apply a downward force on the 1st ray. The clawing is compensation for lack of forefoot pronation and locking of the lateral column. The degree of external tibial torsion and genu valgum suggests compensation from femoral antetorsion. Knowing this fact, and with the presence of a neutral foot progression angle (suggesting adequate compensation of the lower limb torsion to correct the antetorsion), it would be very difficult to place the first ray on the ground effectively without creating greater genu valgus and impacting the opposite knee as it swings past. The diminished midfoot plantar pressures on the left are also in part due to the supinatory compensation of the shorter left limb. It is no surprise that she is developing hallux abducto valgus deformities since there is little anchoring of the first ray on the ground. The anchoring is occurring at the lateral metatarsals and thus drawing the hallux towards their stability. In this case it is a good thing that the midfoot is hypo mobile, otherwise the hallux valgus would be greater.

104

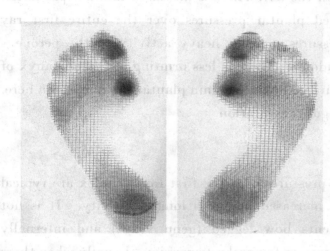

25 YO male runner.
Patient has a 1 month history of bilateral posteromedial ankle pain behind the medial malleolus. The pain is just beginning and is mild. He has had a history of this pain in the past and running avoidance has resolved the pain. There has been no orthotic intervention . The patient runs in a very high cushion, low stability shoe.

The patient is very tender over the peroneal muscle group and over the calcaneocuboid articulation. The soleus is tight and overactive, the gastrocnemius is weak and underactive. There is flexor hallucis longus tenderness and over activity of the extensor digitorum muscles. The FHL tendons are tender posterior to the medial malleolus. The feet are bilaterally forefoot valgus. The midtarsal and forefoot are slightly rigid. Gait evaluation is fairly normal. The knees hinge forward in the saggital plane, there is no excessive pronation but there is a slight genu varus tendency and varus heel posturing.

Comments:

There is a smudge artifact on the left. There is increased midfoot pronation bilaterally. We see increased plantar pressures over the entire first ray complex, L > R. (The pressures indicate heavy activity of the peroneus longus and flexor hallux tendons). There is less printing of the phalanyx of the 5th on the right. There are no lateral column plantar pressures seen here. This is a flexible forefoot valgus presentation.

Discussion:

In this foot type, increased pressures over the first ray complex are typical and this can be driven by increased peroneus longus activity. It is not atypical to see these patients bow legged (genu varus) and internally torsioned in the tibias secondary to femoral retroversion. Usually when there is decreased metatarsal head pressures we will see increased phalangeal pressures as a compensatory gripping to make up for the lack of metatarsal plantar pressures, this patient is just too far medial on the foot. The lack of relative printed lateral pressures (to be precise, there are increased lateral pressures in comparison to medial pressures, but the peroneus longus renders a foci of pressure in it compensation to try and gain purchase on the ground) and increased midfoot pronation suggest that the lateral column is flexible (and that the lateral column joint complex is not locking), hence the tenderness here as the lateral metatarsals dorsiflex as weight bearing loading occurs on the lateral foot. This patient's foot will thus truly not transfer weight effectively over to the medial first ray complex; rather it will toe off laterally. The medial column heat indicates attempts to drop the first ray down to the ground to increase the medial pressures. The rounded lateral foot border from the mid foot into the phalanges is a typical finding on the pedograph for the forefoot valgus presentation. This foot type would benefit

106

from a first ray cut out which would place a slight lift under the lateral metatarsal heads to engage them earlier in terminal stance (by creating earlier calcaneocuboid locking) and the first ray cut out would assist in plantar flexion of the 1st ray. Combined, the lateral lift and the medial drop off level the entire forefoot so that contact during transition from the lateral column to medial is smooth, timely and fluid. This more effective engagement of the lateral column and its locking would reduce the efforts on the peroneus longus and flexor hallucis longus tendons.

The soleus shortness in this case could draw the proximal fibula posterior and when combined with over activation of the peroneus brevis which would draw the distal fibula anterior the next effect is a compromised lateral ankle mortise. Thus stability will be challenged here and with the flexible lateral foot column these patients are at risk for inversion sprains. There are heel artifacts on this graphing, likely from a large stride onto the pedograph.

107

40 YO female with persistent right posterolateral hip and ischeal tuberosity

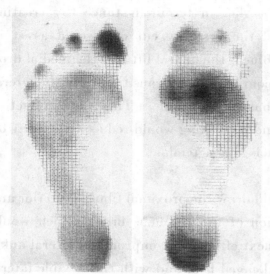

pain of 4 years. *Long distance runner (25 miles weekly). Right posterolateral hip and ischeal tuberosity pain which started in right piriformis area after her 3rd child. Sitting increases her complaint. Right hip and knee "lock up" when the pain begins. She has a sense of an "inability to reach out with her stride during walk and run on the right side".*

Right gluteus medius and maximus inhibition which become easily fatigued. Weak and tight right hamstring (esp. biceps femoris) and overdeveloped hamstrings and quadriceps bilaterally. Deep right hip pain on posterior femoral shear in the acetabulum. Smaller right gluteus on profile. Weak right iliopsoas with a counterclockwise pelvic distortion pattern. Increased rear, mid and forefoot mobility, L>R. Sway back posture, weak right external abdominal obliques. Left limb ~ 4 mm shorter. Running gait evaluation revealed her to be a forefoot striker. There was diminished right hip abductor activation with a left lateral pelvic shift. Heel strike is absent at contact, greater absence on the left. There was a right adductor twist with the heel abruptly internally rotating at heel rise (causing relative external forefoot rotation. There is increased forefoot pronation on the right (long leg side). There is circumduction of the right leg in swing phase and diminished internal hip rotation during stance through heel rise.

Comments:

Increased left FHL activation and clawing of the 2nd digit. There is diminished left heel strike. Diminished right first ray plantar pressures with increased pressures over the 2-3 metatarsals. There is little in the way of right lateral column pressures. There is heavier heel contact on right and less midfoot pronation. There are inadequate right hallux toe off pressures.

Discussion:

This patient is not pronating through the midfoot adequately on the right because she does not have enough internal hip or tibial rotation to shift her weight onto the medial aspect of the foot; this results in greater forefoot pronation, which is complicated by any forefoot varus that may be present. Without heel strike the runner is forced to engage the mid and forefoot more abruptly and with the limb in external rotation and foot in supination (there is no rear to forefoot load transition and thus no transition from tibial external rotation to internal rotation through pronation. In this case there is little right internal limb rotation (she has right anterior femoral glide syndrome which disrupts the posterior femoral head glide thus limiting functional terminal flexion and internal rotation on that side) so she has no choice but to contact the ground as described. Thus, these patients do not effectively engage internal rotation nor is there adequate time to give the external hip rotators much of a chance to eccentrically or isometrically engage to control the internal limb rotation /pronation during contact. Any pronation that does occur does so abruptly and all at once. There will be little use of the shoe's pronatory control devices. Internal rotation of the thigh and lower leg is also limited by the tight hamstrings, causing increased external rotational forces while the right foot is in contact with the ground (recall that the biceps femoris is also an external rotator of the thigh). It is

109

also limiting forward progression of the right limb and shortening her stride length, compared to the left. These 2 factors, along with an uncompensated varus results in greater forefoot imprinting, as we see here. Also remember that the hamstring can be used concentrically during foot stance and mid support phases of running gait, causing increased forefoot pressure, especially in forefoot strikers.

There is diminished heel pressure on the left but this may be a carry-over neurologic pattern from her POSE-like (forefoot strike) running but this is also present due to the short leg; avoiding heel contact will force her more on the forefoot and thus lengthen the limb (note: please take note that the pedograph shows walking plantar pressures and much of our clinical discussion tries to bridge the gap between her walking gait presentation and her troublesome running gait). The increased left flexor hallucis longus activation is there to help her attempt to place more pressure on the medial column to assist her in supinating this shorter left limb. The adductor twist on the right at heel rise indicates shortness of the right hip adductors and right posterior compartment and its cause is likely the inability to achieve adequate internal rotation at the right hip. This caused the shift of the plantar pressures laterally from the first ray onto the 2nd and 3rd metatarsals over which she pivots at toe off. This again is also limited by her ability to compensate in the forefoot due to an uncompensated forefoot varus foot type. Due to the predominant externally rotated position of this limb, the lateral hamstring (B. Femoris) has chronically shortened. When she attempts to run, the increased stride length tugs on the insertion of this muscle and is the cause of her ischeal tuberosity pain at its insertion. This patient also mentioned that she cannot achieve a comfortable reach of the right limb during terminal swing. This is caused by the shortened hamstring

110

and faulty hip biomechanics (inadequate posterior glide of the femoral head during hip flexion causing an impingement of the hip anteriorly during greater hip flexion ranges) caused by a functional syndrome referred to as an *Anterior Femoral Glide Syndrome.*

Anterior Femoral Glide Syndrome is mutifactorially generated but its greatest provoker is the Sway Back posture position. As we mentioned this patient is sway backed. She stands with the pelvis pushed forward in the saggital plane causing a net hip hyperextension.

Sway Back Syndrome:

Patient presents with a posterior orientation of the thoracic center of gravity (t-COG) in relation to the pelvic center of gravity (p-COG). Lordotic changes are variable but are usually hypolordotic and an increased thoracic kyphosis is likely. There is increased thoracic paraspinal muscular development and they are likely stretch weak. The rectus abdominus is likely stretch-weak as are the iliacus and psoas. The hamstrings are typically short drawing the pelvis into posterior rotation. The gluteals are typically underdeveloped and weak. The knee joints are frequently hyper extended (hamstrings actually become dominant knee extensor) and this entire combination of tissue changes forces a stretching of the anterior hip capsule, shortness of the posterior hip capsule and a net anterior shift or glide of the femoral head in the acetabulum.

* It would be a terrible error of omission if we did not mention that a loss of adequate ankle mortise dorsiflexion could also cause the adductor twist of the heel at toe off. As the patient approaches the end range of abbreviated

dorsiflexion they will have no choice but to adduct the heel and flare the foot out into external rotation to achieve a relatively normal step length.

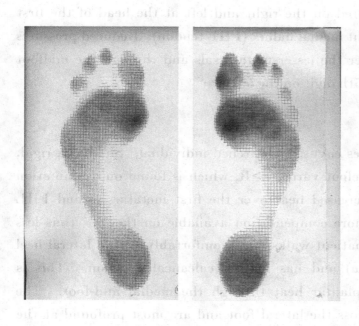

50 YO female with a 10 year history of bilateral lateral and posterolateral ankle discomfort, L>R, during and after long walks.

Examination reveals mild bilateral femoral anteversion with compensatory external tibial torsion. Calcaneal eversion is limited, pronation is minimal (what does occur is mostly mid and forefoot). Genu varus is noted bilaterally. There are Haglund's deformities bilaterally. She has a mild genu recurvatum and reduced ankle dorsiflexion bilaterally. Visually she has high arched cavus feet. There are bilateral, semi-rigid, partially compensated forefoot varus feet. No leg length discrepancy noted.

Gait evaluation showed excessive lateral heel strike and embracing of lateral column plantar pressures. Limited internal limb rotation and pronation was seen. Bilateral medial to lateral (varus) knee shift was apparent just after heel strike. Foot progression angle was greater than 15 degrees. There was a shorter step length with reduced ankle dorsiflexion angle.

Comments:

There is increased heel pressure on the right with some motion artifact at heel strike on the right. Midfoot pronation is limited bilaterally, R>L. Increased

113

plantar pressures were noted on the right and left at the head of the first metatarsals and at the right medial hallux (FHL tendon). Reduced pressures were noted bilaterally over the lesser metatarsals and through the midfoot with no imprinting of the 5th digit on the left.

Discussion:

This patient is a classic pes cavus, high arched individual. She has a rigid, partially compensated forefoot varus, L>R, which is found on examination and confirmed by the increased heat over the first metatarsals and FHL tendons, R>L (there is more compensation available on the left, thus less forefoot pressures). The patient walks most comfortably with a lateral heel strike (calcaneal inversion) and has limited calcaneal eversion. This is denoted by the lack of plantar heat through the medial mid-foot. The pressures come gently across the lateral foot and are most profound at the first metatarsals due to activation of the peroneus longus. This patients clinical symptoms at the posterolateral ankles were as result of the excessive over activity of the peroneus longus in an attempt to bring the medial column (i.e. 1st ray) of the foot to the ground. This patient received notable relief with the application of a 2 degree varus heel posting bilaterally with bilateral forefoot valgus postings. The heel posts reduced the heel strike pronatory stress created by the genu varus and the forefoot posts helped reduce the muscular activity of the peroneii passively helping the forefoot to pronate onto the medial column of the foot.

114

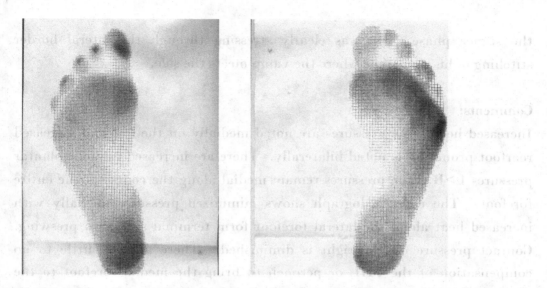

65 YO male with a several year history of right low back pain over the sacroiliac joint.

Examination reveals a ¾ inch leg length discrepancy (short) on the right. He has a ½ inch lift built onto the right sole and a ¼ inch lift built onto the heel of his orthotic. There is weakness of the right lateral hip rotators, and shortening of the right calf musculature. There is tenderness over the right lateral knee joint line. There is a static supinatory tendency of the right foot and pronatory tendency on the left. Static stance showed the right leg externally rotated, abducted, placed slightly forward of the left foot and postured slightly in plantar flexion with increased weight bearing on the forefoot. The right pelvis was lower than the left. During gait this patient exhibited a windswept biomechanical pattern of ambulation. The heel and sole lifts were apparently not satisfactory as the right limb continued to appear shorter. The right limb was planted in abduction and external rotation. The right foot was maintained in a supinatory position throughout the stance phase. He was clearly stressing through the lateral border stitching of his right shoe where the vamp meets the sole.

Comments:

Increased heel strike pressures are noted medially on the left and increased rearfoot pronation is noted bilaterally. There are increased midfoot plantar pressures L>R. The pressures remain medial along the course of the entire forefoot. The right pedograph shows minimized pressures medially with increased heat along the lateral forefoot form terminal stance to preswing. Contact pressure on the right is diminished. There appears little to no compensation of the FHL or peroneii to bring the medial forefoot to the ground on the right. There is heat at the distal insertion of the FHL with evidence of clawing over mets 2-4.

Discussion:

This patient has a windswept pattern of ambulation. He is progressing left to right with increased and prolonged pressures at the heel indicating left calcaneal eversion and thus increased rearfoot pronation and increased medial forefoot pressures on the left and increased at the lateral forefoot on the right. He is obviously pronating more on the left and supinating more on the right. The pain at the right lateral knee is probably secondary to the varus stress at the knee from the significant left to right weight transfer onto the right short leg. The right sacroiliac joint is probably symptomatic due to these varus stresses, from the weakness and overuse of the glutes and hip stabilizers in an attempt to stabilize the joint against the increased forces and from increased sacroiliac joint compression forced when dropping down onto the short leg. We built a slight lift onto the forefoot of his orthotic to try to level out the excessive plantar flexion created by the heel lift. We could not equal the ¼ lift height affixed at the heel due to toe box volume restrictions. For interest sake, we had the patient walk across the pedograph canopy with his shoes on to visualize the gait pressure patterns in the altered shoes. Here we see the same presentation (the shoes have been broken into these patterns). The right shoe shows increased heat over the lateral forefoot and lateral heel. The medial right forefoot is incompletely mapped due to the forefoot supination. The left shoe shows reduced heel printing medially as he has successfully worn through the medial heel of the shoe due to the excessive pronation and is now maintaining the remainder of the plantar pressures over the medial forefoot and FHL area. There is some blurring of the medial forefoot border as on the right side, but for a different reason here. Just as in the left heel mapping he has also worn away the medial aspect of his shoe and thus it does not print well either.

 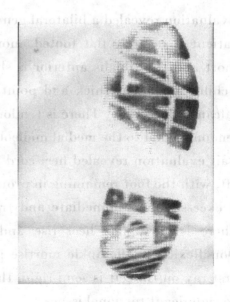

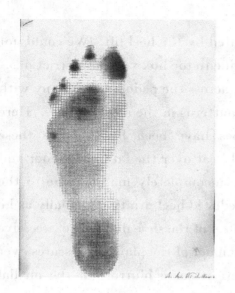 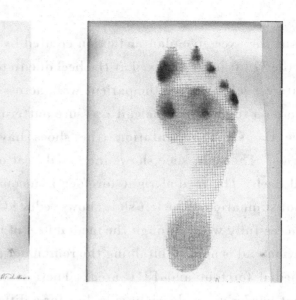

34 YO female security officer with a 6 month history of left achilles pain and swelling.

Evaluation revealed a bilateral genu recurvatum (mild) in static stance. The patient is severely flat footed, more rigid than flexible. The left soleus is short and the tibialis anterior is slightly weaker (than the right). The left Achilles tendon is thick and point tender approximately 1 inch above the calcaneal insertion. There is tendon tenderness along the course of the FHL tendon medial to the medial malleolus. There is no leg length discrepancy.

Gait evaluation revealed heel cord valgus and no calcaneal inversion at heel lift, with the foot remaining in pronation through toe off. Calcaneal eversion is excessive and immediate and translates into hyperpronation bilaterally. There is early left heel rise and a shortened step length on the left. Dorsiflexion of the ankle mortise just prior to heel strike is minimal. The first ray on the left is semi-rigid, the forefoot is varus bilaterally. There are no significant torsional issues.

Comments:

There is increased rearfoot pronation bilaterally, L>R. Midfoot pronation is greater on the left. There are decreased first metatarsal pressures on the left with increased pressure under the halluxes, L>R. Increased plantar pressures are noted under the 2-3 metatarsals bilaterally, greater on the left. The right side exhibits more appropriate 1st metatarsal head pressures. All digits bilaterally have increased plantar pressures indicating clawing. The right side exhibits increased peroneus longus activity to try to improve first ray plantar flexion.

Discussion:

The increased pressures under all digits are compensatory in an attempt to increase intrinsic plantar musculature activity to try to improve metatarsal stability, ground reactive forces as well as arch support. Recall that supination is supposed to be initiated by the contralateral limb entering swing phase and it is dependent on an intact calcaneocuboid locking mechanism, concentric contraction of the anterior and posterior compartments and windlass effect of the plantar fascia. When these mechanisms fail, the peroneus longus acts more as an abductor rather than plantar flexor, which explains the lack of curvature of the lateral border of the print. The tail of the 5th metatarsal is visible on the left! The plantar fascia is insufficient to accomplish the above. The reduced pressures under the first metatarsal are likely secondary to the semi-rigid first metatarsal. The patient has a short soleus secondary to a stretch-weak gastrocnemius on the left. The short soleus is increasing the tendon gain on the Achilles. Remember that there are 4 factors causing heel rise (forward momentum of the body, passive tension in the posterior compartment, active contraction of the posterior compartment and the windlass effect of the plantar fascia.

There is increased tension in the posterior compartment (as evidenced by shortening) and failure of the plantar fascia, along with short weakness of the posterior compartment. The only option for this patient is to try and generate enough strength to assist with heel rise. This, when combined with the hyperpronation effects the Achilles, is frictioning against the sharp medial edge of the calcaneus, with a resultant tendonopathy.

Of incidental note, MRI of the region shows a large os trigonum off of the posterior talus. The os is not osseously fused to the talus; rather there is an area of inflammation at the connection between the two. Large os trigonums are known to friction against the FHL tendon during plantar flexion movements or during sustained dorsiflexion positions (recall this patient is a security officer, riding in a car most of the day with the ankle in dorsiflexion up under the dashboard. Her high riding boots buckle inwards at the region of the Achilles pain and FHL tendon.)

The following cases also have orthotic posting information and clinical pearls which we hope you find helpful.

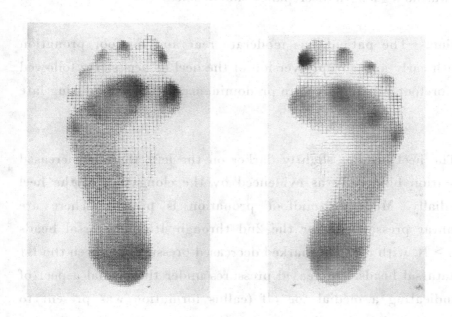

44 YO female runner who complaints of chronic plantar fascitis and medial ankle pain behind the medial malleolus and 2-3 inches above the ankle mortise line immediately behind the tibia. *She has pain at the end of long runs and for the next several days. She has a flexible acrylic orthotic which is unposted at the forefoot or rearfoot. She just transitioned over to Brooks Adrenaline GTS shoes (from a single density soled cushion shoe) to help add more stability for her foot type and for her problems as discussed below.*

Evaluation revealed moderately flexible feet through the mid-tarsal joints. A forefoot varus presentation was noted bilaterally with a very flexible and

121

plantar flexed first ray/metatarsal. Mild hallux valgus formation was evident. There was no evidence of femoral or tibial torsion and no rear foot deformities. There did not appear to be any gross side to side asymmetries. LLD: There was no leg length discrepancy side to side.

Gait Evaluation: The patient has moderate rear and midfoot pronation tendencies with early and abrupt eversion of the heel at heel-strike followed by a medial forefoot plantar pressure predominance in the shoe during late midstance.

Comments: The heel print is slightly darker on the left; there is increased rearfoot pronation bilaterally as evidenced by the elongation of the heel teardrop medially. Moderate midfoot pronation is present. There are increased plantar pressures under the 2nd through 4th metatarsal heads bilaterally, L > R, with a gap of marked decreased pressures between the 1st and 2nd metatarsal heads. Increased pressures under the medial aspect of the hallux indicating a medial toe off (callus formation was present to confirm this). Medial heel strike was noted on the pedograph indicating either a mild degree of calcaneal eversion, a mild internal tibial torsion deformity or evidence of struggles to progress her weight bearing over the first ray complex. In this case, it was due to a more medial heel strike, eversion related.

Orthotic Modifications: This patient has a compensated forefoot varus foot type, (greater on the left); the right is more flexible. In an attempt to assist this foot type a bilateral forefoot first-ray cut-out was utilized. The cut out will allow the first ray to plantar flex comfortably and adequately enough to allow the medial and lateral foot columns to come to rest on the same horizontal plane. This will allow the plantar tissues and intrinsics to function harmoniously and reduce the abnormal biomechanical stressors that were being placed on the tissues since the medial and lateral forefeet were not functioning on the same plane.

Discussion: This is a classic case and pedograph mapping showing the exact mapping one would expect in a Compensated Forefoot Varus foot type with a semi-rigid plantarflexed first metatarsal. She is forefoot varus through the lesser metatarsals but she has compensated fairly well by having the first metatarsal and 1st ray complex semi-flexible and plantarflexed to drop it down to the ground surface to complete the necessary tripod (1st, 5th and heel) for foot stability during stance phase. The crease noted between the 1st and 2nd metatarsal heads is an actual creasing of the plantar skin between these metatarsals. The creasing is because of the plantarflexed first ray. You will often see this longitudinal skin crease on the soles of the feet of more obvious compensated forefoot varus foot type patients.

Clinical Pearl: These patients often have subjective pain in the lower half of the distal calf due to repetitive concentric, isometric, then eccentric strain of the flexor hallucis longus tendon along with the flexor digitorum longus and tibialis posterior. The FHL is overactive in an attempt to synergistically assist in plantarflexion of the first ray complex as well as help to decelerate midfoot pronation during loading response, and midstance.

15 year old tall slender female cross country runner. *Her chief complaint is a 3 year history of right peripatellar knee pain. The knee is always painful and swells mildly following running, but not during running. She runs 40 miles a week in New Balance 900's, a dual density stability shoe.*

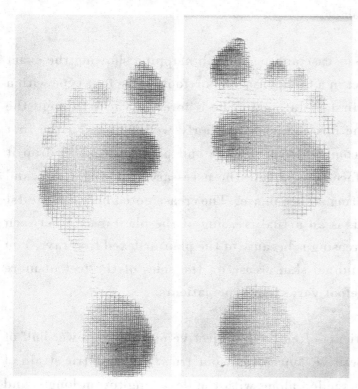

Evaluation revealed bilateral mild genu recurvatum with mild right femoral anteversion and a mild right tibial internal torsion. The left side was neutrally aligned. There was a mild right forefoot varus, neutral on the left. Midfoot flexibility was relatively normal and not excessive. There was a zero degree static-standing foot progression angle as opposed to the more desirable norm of 5-10 degrees. She had moderate forefoot pronation with a moderately accentuated lateral longitudinal arch (calcaneocuboid area to the head of the 5th MT).

LLD: There was no leg length discrepancy (LLD) noted.

Gait evaluation: showed a zero degree left foot progression angle and a negative 5 degree (-5) right foot progression angle. There was a subtle right limb internal rotation as the lower limb advanced into knee extension preparing for heel strike (there is an interesting last moment lateral foot progression flare at the moment before heel strike to try to re-align the internally rotated-torsioned right limb and foot). There was a sudden but mild internal "checking" of the right patella at heel contact.

Comments: The pedograph shows medial heel strike bilaterally, L > R with little if any midfoot pressures. There are medial forefoot pressures and mild lateral forefoot pressures with accentuation of the 5th. This is an interesting pedograph mapping. One would expect that a moderate pronator would have more plantar pressures at the medial arch pedograph printing. In cases when there are mild to moderate amounts of midfoot pronation available, and particularly when there is internal tibial torsion, the pedograph will confirm that when walking the foot will print heavier medially at the heel as it will strike here first. The forces then attempt to remain medial because of the internal tibial torsion but this is not always possible in higher degrees of internal tibial torsion. In the more aggressive torsional cases the patient is forced to toe off laterally since the first ray of the foot is turned in too far medially. This more lateral progression creates the void in medial plantar mapping pressures. Additionally, when the internal torsion is great enough, the peroneii can be tensioned creating a lift in the lateral arch at the midfoot (calcaneocuboid interval) creating the void in lateral pressures as noted on this pedograph. If these clients shifted laterally they would put the foot in an unstable position and run the risk of an inversion sprain.

During running these patients will quite frequently avoid heel strike to avoid the increased torsional stressors on the limb as the foot is forced to more quickly internally torsion to bring the foot to the ground. They also avoid heel strike because they cannot achieve enough external-lateral hip rotation to achieve a full unlimited forward step and stride length, thus they eliminate the heel strike of the contact phase allowing them to remain in the stride phase a little longer and thus achieve a longer step-strike length.

Additionally, if they did heel strike they would most certainly have to toe off ineffectively laterally off of the lateral digits. This would be a most ineffective gait cycle. This is one of the reasons why internally torsioned patients may have a difficult time running. The sudden torsion from initial contact to midstance can place undue stress upon the knees and because the significant internal hip stressors can cause labral-acetabular problems like dysplasia as seen in Acetabular Rim Syndrome. These patients, if they choose to run, should be retrained to have a midfoot strike and they would often benefit from a highly cushioned shoe. In more mild cases, if they do heel strike and choose to run, they should choose a shoe that has a very soft lateral heel ("crash zone") and an abbreviated crash entry-zone cut out to help them stay more lateral in the rear-foot a little longer. This should translate into delayed subtalar joint pronation, reduced internal torsion acceleration and lessened medial foot pressures.

Orthotic Modifications: Since her existing full arch contact orthotic was not sufficient to control midfoot pronation, we glued a 2mm thermocork forefoot wedge onto her shoe inserts liner. The wedge was a varus wedge, lifting the first ray complex to bring the lateral and medial forefoot onto the same functional plane. The wedge was tapered to non-existence laterally. This addition translates into bringing the ground up to the foot earlier than what it is used to doing. This means less foot pronation and thus less internal tibial torsion.

Clinical Pearl: The key to getting this posting correct is a fine line, too much or too little posting correction means magnifying the torsional stress at the tibia-femoral joint junction and undue stresses on the knee. These patients often have patello femoral tracking and meniscal problems and need improved coordination and eccentric strength of the quadriceps extensor mechanism.

55 YO male complaining of bilateral pain between the 3rd - 4th and 4th – 5th toes. *He has had this complaint for several months. The pain is worse during gait.*

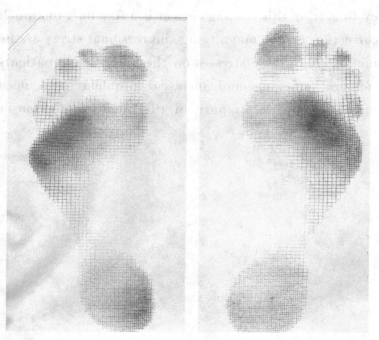

On examination there are small red irritated corns at the corresponding medial and lateral aspects of the IP joints. The ankle mortise range of motion is limited but adequate to allow normal mortise function. There is a bilateral rigid 1st metatarso- phalangeal joint, he has roughly 20° dorsiflexion bilaterally at this joint. There is no hallux abducto valgus. Forefoot varus is obviously noted bilaterally. A small but defined callus is noted at the medial aspect of the hallux bilaterally.

Gait evaluation: reveals an adductor twist of the heels at heel lift. He appears to be using a hip flexor strategy at toe off (see discussion below). Stride and step lengths appear to be shorter than this individual might normally and easily engage. This patient walked with an accentuated foot progression angle.

LLD: There was no leg length discrepancy (LLD) noted on examination.

Comments: Pedograph mapping reveals increased heel pressure medially on the left. Little midfoot pressures are noted. There are increased pressures over metatarsals 2-4 with a marked lack of the 1st ray plantar pressures. Stride measurement is significantly shortened from normal for this gentleman's physical stature.

Discussion: In this case the patient's pain is coming from the friction that is occurring from the abnormal pressures generated during stance phase, particularly toe-off. Since the patient is avoiding 1st ray toe-off pressures at the forefoot because of the forefoot varus foot type, contact is occurring medial to lateral creating a torsional movement, or spinning moment, around the second and third and/or third and fourth metatarsals. (We sometimes describe this type of gait as a "skating-like" gait in which the patient is essentially using the same mechanics as one would if they were skating in a straight line. Push off appears to be medial but since medial pressure on the rigid 1st toe is not effective, due to pain, push off occurs as the foot abuts the lateral aspect of the inside of the shoe. In others words, it is as if the foot slides laterally in the shoe until it hits the lateral shoe / vamp wall, at which time forces are then translated into the shoe. These types of patients frequently will "blow out" the lateral stitching of a shoe where it meets the sole and they may even appear to stand and walk on the lateral aspect of the shoe at all times.) As this torsion occurs, (for example the right foot will be undergoing a clockwise torsioning) the third metatarsal would be moving

129

forward and the fourth metatarsal would be moving backwards. (In actual fact the more lateral toe would be somewhat fixed by its contact with the lateral aspect of the shoe's toe box creating a more fixed base on which the more medial toe can rub forward upon. This phenomenon will occur more frequently in a narrower, pointed or tight toe box where the toes are approximated by reduce toe-box volume. This friction between the sides of the IP joints create an irritation and callusing effect and hence the painful corns. The twist of the heel at heel lift is what initiates this clockwise torsioning effect on the right heel and counterclockwise in the left.

To resolve this patient's problem and get to a reasonable toe-off position they must achieve more dorsiflexion either at the metatarsal-cuneiform joint, ankle mortise or at the hip by increasing flexion (the "hip flexion strategy"). As the patient reaches the terminal hallux limitus dorsiflexion range which is available to them, they must achieve these extra ranges at the above mentioned joints. The only means of doing this is to incorporate the Hip Flexor Strategy. This patient will improperly use the iliopsoas as the hip flexion initiator as opposed its normal function as a hip flexion perpetuator. This patient will have less pelvic obliquity as a result of the short step length which will initiate early heel rise and the adductor twist. To gain enough forward momentum of the limb, which could not be achieve by the pelvic obliquity, the hip flexor is recruited to also perform initial hip flexion in the early swing phase instead of its normal function as a hip flexion perpetuator during mid to late swing phase.

Clinical Pearl: Correction for this patient requires a rocker bottom shoe, a rigid Morton's extension applied to the orthotic, and/or cushioned to toe spacer's for the corns. The cushioned spacers are "band aids" for the corns but maximizing of the 1st metatarso phalangeal dorsiflexion range of motion is the key. The problem is doing so within painless limits and not overloading the joint so that further pain or osteoarthritic change is not created at the joint. These types of foot biomechanics can also be the cause of Morton's neuromas, due to the lateral displacement of pressures and resultant friction between the adjacent metatarsals.

10 YO young man has just recently come out of a short leg cast for a Right tri-malleolar ankle fracture.

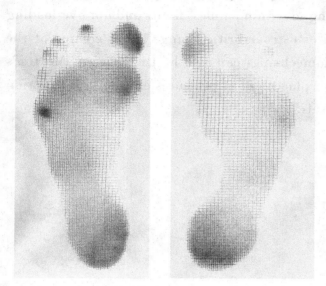

He was casted in relative ankle mortise neutral for 8 weeks, the last 2 of which he was in a rocker bottom boot for ambulation purposes. He has 2 implanted screws through the distal tibia-fibular syndesmosis due the separation injury that occurred between the tibia and fibula.

Examination: Moderate ankle edema and thickened Achilles tendon. There is tenderness over the distal tibia-fibula syndesmosis and over the anterior ankle mortise joint. Only 90 degrees of ankle mortise dorsiflexion is achieved. There is no evidence of femoral or tibial torsioning. Rear and mid foot inversion and eversion are limited as a result of the edematous tissues and lack of subtalar motion. There is marked weakness of the right gastroc soleus complex with notable shortening of both muscles. The quadriceps are also significantly weak.

LLD: There was no leg length discrepancy.

Gait Evaluation: There is a significant limping gait favoring the right limb. He is ambulating with the foot and limb externally rotated. He shies away from full right limb weight bearing. He cannot toe off normally, his strategy

132

is to roll off of the foot medially once he hits the ankle mortise barrier at 90 degrees, he also partially uses the Hip Hiking Strategy and Hip Flexor Strategy as discussed in the section under Ankle Dorsiflexion previously in this text.

Comments: Pedograph reveals increased medial heel pressures bilaterally, R > L. There are significantly reduced mid and forefoot plantar pressures on the right. There is little toe contact and no effective toe off of the right medial column. There is heat beneath the head of the 5th met on the left.

Discussion: Heel strike is the only time this patient significantly employs the right foot. As he approaches midstance, he shifts his weight laterally and to the left, as evidenced by the printing of the tail (base) of the 5th metatarsal and head of the 5th. He claws with toes 2-4 to improve propulsion and also employs the FHL to assist in forward progression. The Hip Flexor Strategy will eventually place undue stress on the iliopsoas and other hip structures. If ankle mortise dorsiflexion range is not restored quickly this patient may need some therapy on the hip for subsequent compensatory problems. This patient has already developed posterior hip joint capsule retraction and shortening of the glutes and short external hip rotators. Low back pain is not far off in our estimation. If the dorsiflexion range at the right ankle is never achieved one could expect that the right foot will increase its midtarsal pronation (and probably external rotation of the right lower extremity to assist in gaining purchase on the ground and create a rigid lever) resulting in an eventual flatter foot development (acquired pes planus) and with it possible plantar fascial and tibialis posterior problems.

Clinical Pearls: Graded mobilizations are critical in this case. The restricted ankle dorsiflexion range is keeping the soleus shut down. This will need to be addressed once the range is restored otherwise the patient may over utilize the gastrocnemius, tibialis posterior, or the flexor digitorum synergists to compensate, thus leading to further problems. It should be clear to the reader that when one joint is compromised the body will compensate but that these compensations, if left unaddressed, will result in secondary problems biomechanically and symptomatically. This patient may also begin to develop some knee pain, either anteriorly in the peripatellar region due to quadriceps weakness and malcoordination or at the anterior tib-femoral joint line secondary to the sustained "straight legged – peg-legged" gait. Posterior knee pain may be due to capsular stretching and the hyperextension tendency afforded by his present gait pattern.

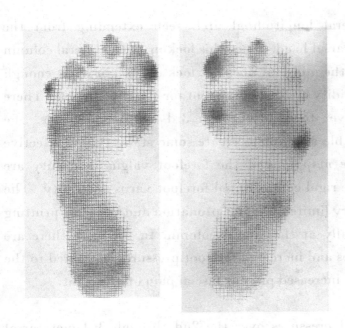

45 YO female triathlete and runner with chronic plantar fasciitis (right greater than left) and right metatarsalgia over the 2nd through 4th metatarsal heads. *She is a short, stocky woman. She runs in Asics Gel Kayanos with a custom made full contact orthotic. The orthotic is presently unposted.*

Examination: Normal gait step and stride length. She is very flexible at the midtarsal joints. She has a flexible is forefoot valgus bilaterally. She has prominent Morton's type feet, longer second metatarsal and digit. Her feet are flat and hyperpronated. No torsional deformities.

LLD: There are no changes in leg length discrepancy side to side.

Gait Evaluation: Nothing notable other than obvious increased pronation and splay of the foot during all contact phases.

Comments: There is increased pronation at the rearfoot, midfoot and forefoot. There is prominent pressure mapping of the 5th metatarsal styloid-base and heads bilaterally, R > L. This is quite frequently seen in flexible forefoot valgus feet. Its presence on a mapping suggests that the forefoot is so flexible and valgus that the 5th metatarsal cannot be plantarflexed creating the normal lateral longitudinal arch seen extending from the calcaneus to the 5th metatarsal head. Since this locking of the lateral column does not occur effectively the mid-foot does not lock enough or early enough and hence there is little rigidity created in the foot for effective toe-off. There are increased pressures over the 2nd through 3rd metatarsal heads. She employs the FHL in a feeble attempt to create some stability and effective lever for ambulation. The mappings of the forefoot valgus deformity are quite similar to that of the rigid compensated forefoot varus deformity. The latter will usually have very limited midfoot pronation and thus less printing on the pedograph, especially at the lateral column. In this case there are reduced right heel pressures and increased forefoot pressures compared to the left, as expected due to the increased plantar fascial pain on the right.

Discussion: The increased pressures over the 2nd through 3rd metatarsal heads are indicative of a foot that cannot maintain or transfer forces over the first ray for efficient toe-off. The reduced right heel pressures and increased forefoot pressures, as compared to the left, are likely a causative compensation and the source of the metatarsalgia pain on this side.

Orthotic modifications: A rearfoot varus post, to help further control and delay midfoot pronation is especially helpful in these cases. Lifting of the arch of the orthotic will help supinate the foot and enable earlier locking of the calcaneocuboid joint thus reducing the degree of forefoot valgus deformity. A triangular thermocork forefoot valgus wedge (post) can also be helpful, wedged thick to thin, lateral to medial respectively but not extending under the 1st metatarsal head. We extended the posting back to the lateral heel to fill the gap in the orthotic that was created by the longitudinal arch when the feet were casted.   The orthotic was unstable laterally as a result of this gap, as are most orthotics. (There is frequently a gap laterally between the heel and 5th metatarsal area of the orthotic formed by a lateral arch. The lateral arch can be normal but if the orthotic is not constructed properly as the patient transitions from lateral heel strike to lateral forefoot, an unstable lateral orthotic will tip the patient laterally or keep them lateral too long. This will affect normal foot progression during gait. Thus, we filled this lateral arch gap with thermocork to make the entire orthotic stable laterally.) Finding an orthotic that engages the entire lateral plantar aspect of the orthotic flush with the ground or shoe surface so that this issue of lateral instability cannot even come into play is key.

Clinical Pearls: Quite frequently clinicians and patients alike believe that metatarsalgia pain is a result of not enough cushioning at the forefoot. This can be the case in a patient who had atrophied their metatarsal fat pads but it quite frequently can be the result of abnormal forefoot pressures secondary to a forefoot deformity, as in this case, forefoot valgus variation bilaterally. It is confirmatory to note that in this case the patient had very thick and prominent metatarsal fat pads. A more logical approach is to raise the arch to achieve more supination and lateral column locking and, if necessary, apply a forefoot valgus posting on the orthotic.

Postlude:

We hope you enjoyed reading our book as much as we enjoyed putting it together. Hopefully, we have created questions in your mind, not only about our sanity and nerdiness, but about foot evaluation and gait analysis, and perhaps, opened new doors for you. We hope to see you in airports staring at peoples gait and looking at people's feet in the line at the grocery store. When we do, we will smile, knowing that we have somehow worked our way into your inferior temporal gyrus and you will never be quite the same, or look at the world without thinking about its foundation and what profound effects occur in compensation to the way we interact with the earth's gravitational field. If we have done our job, you will pester shoe manufacturers to do a better job and have running clinics in your neighborhood. Most of all we hope you will help us to help this book evolve, as it is only the beginning...

See you in the shoe isle.

Ivo and Shawn